ONE *who* UNITES
HEAVEN *and* EARTH

ONE
who
UNITES
HEAVEN
and
EARTH

The Autobiography of
MASAHISA GOI

BYAKKO PRESS

ISBN 13: 978-4-89214-166-9
ISBN 10: 4-89214-166-6

Published by Byakko Press
812-1 Hitoana, Fujinomiya, Shizuoka, Japan 418-0102
http://www.byakkopress.ne.jp
E-mail: e-info@byakkopress.ne.jp

Printed and distributed by Booksurge.com
7290-B Investment Drive, N. Charleston, SC, USA 29418
Tel. 1-843-853-8310; toll free 1-866-308-6235
http://www.booksurge.com
E-mail: info@booksurge.com

Originally published as *Ten to chi o tsunagu mono*
(天と地をつなぐ者), Byakko Press, 1955.

Managing editor and translator: Mary L. McQuaid
Translated by Kinuko Hamaya, Erina Kobayashi, Akiko
Stevenson, Fumi Stewart, Shunsuke Takagi, Noriko Tatsuma, and
Sonoko Tanaka. Consulting translator: Judith L. Hunt.
Consulting editor: Hisashi Goto.
Editing and book design by David W. Edelstein.

Cover photo and design by Mariana Chiarella.
E-mail: foto@marianachiarella.com

Contents

Preface...7

Childhood, Part I..10

Childhood, Part II...17

My Youth...26

Seeking the Divine Self..44

The Divine Plan..75

Shedding the Old Self...102

Communicating with Spiritual and
Subconscious Worlds..118

Departing from the Realistic World...............................133

The Trials of Spiritual Training.....................................144

Approaching Perfect Spiritual Freedom........................168

Heaven and Earth Become One......................................176

Notes..204

A Message to Our Readers...210

Preface

"A human being is a small universe." I remember hearing these words from someone when I was a small boy, and now I can really nod in agreement with them. It is indeed true that the universe reflects its principles through the paths that we human beings are walking along; but the question is, does our way of living express the universal heart in a true or a distorted manner? The answer depends on whether our steps are true or false, beautiful or ugly.

And so, as we each walk along our own path in life, it makes a big difference whether we live only as physical beings, or as spiritual beings as well. This is what determines the beauty or the ugliness in a human being's way of living.

In this book, I write about my own spiritual journey,

just the way it unfolded. And in looking back on these events, I find that I was a person who could not help but place greater emphasis on the spiritual than on the physical side of life. Indeed, it would not have been possible for me to live in any other way.

Through my own real experience, I became clearly aware that the physical body is one of the vessels of the spirit. I realized that a human being is essentially spirit, and that the spirit works within the physical body via our thought vibrations and our physical elements combined.[1]

I realized, too, that the spirit—our true being—is divine life itself, acting in accordance with the movement of the great universal life, or universal God. Through my own experience, I also recognized that from second to second and moment to moment, each human being exerts an influence on the vast universe. Words cannot begin to describe the importance of one human being's existence.

I also came to know that this human world can turn into either a heaven or a hell, depending on the beliefs that human beings live by. When we live believing that humans are material existences and nothing else, we cause a world of hell to take shape around us; and when we live believing that our physical being is a workplace for God and spirit, we cause heaven to manifest itself on earth. Truth, goodness, and beauty do not spring from the physical body. Rather, these qualities find expression in the body when the soul approaches closer to God and acquires a deeper love for humanity.

I would not encourage others to take the road that I have travelled, for each person has his or her own individual path in life. My wish is for each person to live with dignity in the way that suits them best, and to progress along their own path without losing their way, always praying to the inner divine self.

The title of this book, *One Who Unites Heaven and Earth*, came about through my spiritual experience of uniting my divine (heavenly) self with my physical (earthly) consciousness. It is my hope that, in reading this book, even a few more people may recognize that, by nature, all human beings are able to do the same.

> Forms naturally appear and disappear
> In the world around me.
> I simply remain
> In crystalline quietness.
>
> My body is in this world
> But my life is joined with the Infinite,
> Shining on heaven and earth.

Masahisa Goi
June 1955

Childhood, Part I

I was born in Tokyo, in the district of Asakusa, some time between five and six o'clock on the evening of November 22, 1916.

My father was descended from a samurai family which, during the feudal age, served the Nagaoka clan of Echigo Province. At the entrance to our home there was always a nameplate, specially placed by my father, reading: "Manjiro Goi of samurai descent."

Full of hopes and dreams, my father had left his hometown at the age of fifteen or sixteen and moved to Tokyo to seek his fortune. Yet, being prone to illness and having many children, he was obliged to spend his entire life at an occupation that never gladdened his heart. His sole source of pride seemed to be the nameplate that attested to his samurai heritage.

My mother, Kiku, the daughter of a merchant, was born in Tokyo. Her qualities of toughness and dynamism enabled her to support her ailing husband and give birth to nine children, eventually raising eight of us, two girls and six boys, to adulthood.

Although I was only little at the time, I remember well that she used to run a tiny candy shop at home, and sometimes did hairdressing there too. "Never borrow money from anyone. No matter how tough things get, you must get through it on your own." This was the constant litany that we heard from our mother. And in keeping with her words, my mother's greatest source of pride lay in the fact that no matter how difficult our life became, she never borrowed a cent from anyone. For this reason, only my eldest brother attended school with my parents' financial assistance. The rest of us had to work our way through school. However, none of us resented this, because we had grown up seeing how hard our mother worked from morning till night, hardly even sparing time for sleep.

Like my father, I had poor health when I was little. As I grew into boyhood, doctors frequently doubted whether I would survive to adulthood. When physical check-ups were held at school, I remember the doctors and teachers craning their necks to look at my body as they pointed to it and described it as a typical example of an infirm constitution. In hushed tones they commented that it would be a wonder of medical science if I grew up without succumbing to tuberculosis.

I listened silently to such whispered exchanges, overcome by an indescribable feeling of something between fear and pain. Perhaps because of this, I felt extremely reluctant to undress in front of others, and I absolutely loathed going to the public baths. At the same time, I started to give up hope on ever having good health, for I felt that I was sure to die of tuberculosis or some sort of stomach or intestinal disorder by the time I reached adulthood, if not sooner.

Before I knew it, I found myself becoming seriously interested in the subject of death. I think this must have been the first step in the awakening of my philosophical and religious turn of mind.

Despite my misgivings about my health, hidden deep in my heart there was an element of cheerfulness and optimism that did not accord with the frail state of my body. I often performed comical dances for the amusement of my mother and my brothers and sisters. It didn't matter to me if they considered me silly and foolish. Just seeing their enjoyment made me happy.

From childhood, I entertained myself by reading

books and singing songs. Composition and singing were my favorite subjects at school, and I was often praised for my clear, strong pronunciation in reading texts—even by the school principal himself. I think the reasons for my becoming a musician at one point had a lot to do with what I experienced during that period.

I was a fine-featured, pale-faced child with angular shoulders, a sunken chest, and short stature. Even so, I did not project a gloomy image to others. This was due to my affable disposition and ever-present smile. One thing that I could never bear was to give an unpleasant feeling to others. I seem to have gone to great lengths never to hurt people's feelings or make them feel bad. I think that, with the passage of time, this turned into a habit and gave me the natural ability to see into people's hearts, so that, without the slightest effort, I could always speak and behave in ways that would not hurt people's feelings.

To me, it was always preferable to lose something than to gain it by harming others. There was no particular reasoning behind this. It simply felt like the most natural way to behave.

After the fire that raged in the wake of the Great Kanto Earthquake of 1923, we were left homeless and without possessions, and were living in emergency barracks with only the clothes on our backs. One day at school, donations coming from various parts of the country were distributed to us children who had suffered from the earthquake. Among the donated articles, the most valuable items were the clothing. However, there was not enough clothing to be distributed to all the students. The teacher then said: "Any students who have no clothing other than what you are wearing now, please raise your hands." Almost all the children raised their hands. Only I and two or three other students kept our hands down. I did not raise my hand because I remembered that, besides the shirt I was wearing at the moment, I had another that had been given to me by relatives in the interior.

I returned home thinking it only natural that I had not been given anything. That day, donated items had apparently been distributed in the other schools too, and all my older brothers and sisters had received clothing. Upon seeing that I had come home empty-handed, my mother said: "Didn't they give out any clothing at your school?"

"They did, but I told them I had another shirt at home, so I didn't receive any," I replied.

Hearing this, my mother exclaimed: "I can't believe my ears! Here was a chance to get another article of clothing, and... What a shame! This child is hopeless!" As she spoke, she looked at me in utter dismay.

Upon hearing those words, I suddenly began to think that perhaps I was indeed a foolish child. I knew that all the students who had raised their hands had gone home with clothing. Among them were boys from well-to-do families. I felt absolutely disconsolate and hung my head before my mother. I was ready to cry if she said another word.

Happily, my mother uttered no further words of reproach. In her eyes, I must have seemed a sadly stupid child who, with but one other shirt to his name, thought nothing of rejecting a precious gift of clothing.

For quite some time this incident lingered in my youthful mind as an unresolved problem. Was I honest, or was I an honest fool? It took quite some time before I reached the conclusion that I had acted in the only way that was possible for me at the time. Then, and only then, did my heart become light again.

In childhood, physical frailty was not my only problem. Ever since my first year in school, my left eyelid had been red and swollen and always looked inflamed. I applied various types of remedies to it and bandaged it, but this only accentuated my unwell appearance and made me look even more frail. Though examined by various doctors, the inflammation refused to heal. Looking back on it now, it seems to me that both my eye condition and my frail physique must have been a means for purifying the erroneous thoughts, or karma, of my ancestors.

These various infirmities had the effect of subduing

my naturally bright and vibrant nature, turning me into a person who related more with the inner self than with the external world. In other words, it naturally led to my taking an interest in the affairs of the soul.

Childhood, Part II

I don't know if it was because my family was poor, but I remember that, starting from the age of three or so, I sometimes thought about my future livelihood, wondering what kind of life I should lead and what kind of work would suit me best. Whenever I was called 'Botchan' by grown-ups who did not know me, I would think to myself, "No, you are mistaken. I am not Botchan." 'Botchan' was what people called little boys from wealthy families. To my way of thinking, it was not fitting for a child from a poor family like mine to be addressed in that way.

I remember vaguely feeling that I would need to become independent and earn my own living as soon as I could. Nevertheless, I bore no antipathy toward the rich, no jaded view on life ever took shape in my young mind. The psychology of self-reliance was just something that came naturally to me.

Starting with my first year at elementary school, my cap, clothing, bag, and books were all hand-me-downs from my elder brothers. I remember that having the answers to the questions all neatly written in the textbooks was very useful to me in my studies.

The Great Kanto Earthquake, which happened on September 1, 1923, seems to have been the first event that changed the course of my life. This was because the earthquake was followed by a fire that destroyed our home, and my uncle—the husband of my father's sister—came to see us from my father's home town in Echigo (now Niigata Prefecture). After spending some time with my family, my uncle took me back with him to Echigo. This gave me the opportunity to see my father's homeland for the very first time.

Without a doubt, the life I led in Echigo was a great source of strength to me, in both body and soul. This was because, as I later realized, there was during that period a profound interaction going on between me and the enlightened spirits of my ancestors. I stayed in Echigo until the end of second grade, when I was eight. I spent much of that year communing with nature, and even after returning to Tokyo I would go back nearly every summer to

18

Echigo, the homeland of my father's ancestors. There, I became more and more at home with the world of nature.

Niigata-ken, Koshi-gun Kamigumi-mura, Aza-Yoko-makura: this was the name of the place where my father's elder sister had her home. The home of his younger brother was located in the community now known as Tōka-machi, in the city of Nagaoka. I would spend about one-tenth of the time at my uncle's home, and the rest at the home of my aunt. While staying with my aunt's family I would get up early each morning and climb the small mountain that was behind the house. There, I would play and gather firewood for my aunt. I can still see myself now, huffing and puffing as I climbed down the mountain with a load of firewood on my back.

Even though my aunt had two sons of her own, she showered me with as much affection as she did them. I idolized my cousins, just as if they had been my own big brothers, and was delighted whenever they invited me to play with them. If I had been in Tokyo, where I had three older and two younger brothers and sisters living at home, I would rarely have had the chance to do as I liked; but in Echigo, everyone tried to please me and I felt quite free.

When I reflect on it now, it seems like the most natural thing in the world that, in those days, I liked temples. I loved going to the Jōshōin temple, which was up on the mountain behind the house, and listening to the chant-

19

ing of the Buddhist sutras and the sounds of the wooden gongs. When I was a little older, I would sit alone in the temple garden practicing *zazen* (seated meditation) and meditating on oneness with my divine self. I understand now that I was guided through all these experiences by the enlightened spirits of my ancestors. This must be why I had such a deep and close feeling for Echigo. It seemed like more of a home to me than Asakusa in Tokyo, the place where I was actually born.

Whenever I was in Tokyo, the question of how to make ends meet was always in the forefront, reminding me of the need to become financially independent as soon as I could. I did not have that exuberant feeling that comes when life really shines. My heart always felt weighed down by the pressing need to become self-supporting.

Both my father and mother wanted each of us brothers to become independent as quickly as possible, and they were not at all concerned with our achieving what other people considered 'success in life.' I think I was very lucky, because I did not have to anticipate any future duties toward my parents during their old age. I was free to do as I chose, and to aspire to whatever I liked.

Ever since primary school I had enjoyed composing poetry in the traditional Japanese styles of *tanka* and *haiku*,[2] and in composition I always ranked first or second in the class. I was also good at singing. It was my wish at the time to become a writer, a musician, or a teacher; however, all those professions required lengthy study.

Because I was only a child, I doubt that I understood much of the meaning, but I was an avid reader of both Japanese and world literature. I also read novels by an author called Koroku Sato, which at that time were very popular among young boys. I was fascinated by these books, whose heroes served as models for how to grow up as a worthy person or a great man. Fortified by these examples, I resolved to go out into the world with courage, and make the most of my life by studying and working hard.

After completing my first year of junior high school, I took a job as an apprentice in a small wholesale textile shop called the T Store, which had advertised for a junior assistant. This fit perfectly with my plans to strengthen my body and spirit by working and studying at the same time. Knowing that a junior high education would not suffice for making my way in the world, I firmly resolved to get a higher education and make myself useful to others. And so it was that a small boy of thirteen, weighing the least in his school, stepped out into the world like one of the heroes of the Koroku Sato novels, his heart brimming over with hopes for the future.

We live-in apprentices at the T Store had to get up early in the morning, as did the live-in maids, and share in the cleaning of the whole house. We would then put everything in the shop in order before the arrival of the clerks, who commuted from their own residences. The work was fine in summertime but unbearable in the winter, because the water was freezing cold. Even so, I was firmly determined to work hard and build up my health while studying, so as to grow up to be a worthy person.

Because, unlike the others, I did not aspire to become a merchant, I felt that I ought to be doing something extra. I decided to get up at four o'clock, while the others were still sleeping. I would clean the carts and sweep the street outside the shop, then study as much as I could before the others got up.

Whenever I encountered an unpleasant situation, I used the experience to invigorate myself and purify my heart and spirit, and this kept me feeling light-hearted and motivated from day to day. At first I found it tremendously hard to walk from Nihonbashi to somewhere like Nerima,[3] pulling the cart behind me. When walking uphill or on an asphalt road that was melting in the summer heat I had to pull the cart with all my might. Otherwise, the wheels would get stuck in the road, and would not move even one inch forward or backward. This was because the cart was loaded with boxes filled with rolls of textiles. It was exceedingly hard work for a thirteen-year-old boy with a slighter-than-average physique.

In those days, I think I really experienced what Ieyasu Tokugawa[4] meant when he said: "Life is like walking a long way with a heavy load on your back." When walking uphill, pulling a cart behind you, at the beginning you can glance up at the top, but after that the best thing is to advance step by step looking only at your feet. If you get distracted and look up even for a second, you can end up sliding down the road. It is exactly the same with life. You can hold a lofty ideal, but in daily life it is important to move steadily forward, step by step. Those who only pursue their ideals are likely to fall by the wayside and drive their families into misery.

Here is a poem that I wrote in those days:

With my hands and feet
Frozen and painful
I have a long way to go
On the road ahead.

In those days, my daily routine was to get up at four in the morning, pull the cart in the daytime, attend class in the evening, read books at night, and go to bed around midnight. Sometimes this was difficult to maintain, though. It often happened that I did not have free time at night because I had to work overtime. So, to make up for the class I had missed, I would study in the daytime while pulling the cart.

Once I had grown accustomed to pulling the cart, it was not so hard for me to study my English textbook and pull the cart at the same time. Since there were scarcely any automobiles on the road, I hardly needed to pay attention to traffic. Over time I had mastered the art of pulling so well that on sunny days I could simply lean my body against the handles, shift my weight forward, and the cart would move ahead naturally. As my eyes followed the printed words in the textbook, I felt that my thirst for knowledge was being satisfied, and my heart knew the joy of being truly alive.

By and by, I was promoted to the rank of salesman, and began to do my rounds on a bicycle. I then had the freedom to arrange my own working hours, and could even find time to practice judo in the mornings. I was growing wonderfully healthy in both mind and body. It seemed to me that the improvement in my health was due not only to hard labor, but also to the yoga-like breathing and meditation that I practiced before going to bed each night. I cannot recall how I learned it, but I had been steadily doing it since I was thirteen years old.

I could spare a lot of time for reading because I could manage my own time, and this made me happier than anything else. I hunted for second hand books, and in addition to works of literature and philosophy I also read the Bible and the Buddhist scriptures.

I was not looking for rote knowledge, but wanted to find in books and music such words and deeds as would resonate in the depths of my mind. I did not plan this out systematically. It seemed that some unknown power was naturally guiding me from within.

When I was eighteen or nineteen, I left my job at the T Store and became independent, opening the Goi Commercial Establishment, which dealt in both wholesale and retail sales. I was both owner and clerk at the same time. It was during this period that I began my formal music studies. However, while studying music, I felt that becoming a teacher or a writer might be the most suitable path for me. I wanted to work at something that would benefit humankind, and this desire was growing deeper and stronger.

I think it was around that time that I began to take part in poets' circles,[5] and I also tried to write a novel.

My Youth

I completed my musical studies while working at the same time. For a while, I gave music lessons to young students. Then, in September of 1940, through an introduction from one of my brothers, I was hired by the Kameari factory, a subsidiary of the Hitachi Manufacturing Group.

My brother Toshio was an electrical technician and had been working for Hitachi for a long time. One day, during a conversation with Mr. Kunio Yagi, who was in charge of employee well-being for the Personnel Department, Toshio happened to mention my musical experience. In reply, Mr. Yagi said, "Actually, I am thinking of starting a broad-based cultural initiative, and would like to find a choral instructor. Do you think you could bring your brother to meet me?"

When Toshio came home and told me about his conversation with Mr. Yagi, I immediately felt that this might be a good opportunity for me. I had entered the field of music because I loved it very much, but studying and working at the same time had proven to be very difficult.

Also, it had become clear to me that in order to become a first-rate musician one had to possess rare talent. With my short fingers, I wasn't really cut out to be a pianist. And without instrumental ability, I felt it would be too difficult for me to pursue my aim of becoming a composer.

Thus, I found myself obliged to choose the only option left—singing, or vocal music. Fortunately, I had a fairly good voice, and my teacher frequently expressed high expectations for me as a high-baritone singer. Still, I never liked the flamboyance of singing onstage and I lacked the confidence to pursue a career as a professional singer and performer. This lack of confidence was partly due to insufficient effort and practice. Also, at that stage in my life I considered the work of vocalists to be less meaningful than that of composers and instrumentalists, and this thinking might have influenced my decision.

In reflecting on the situation, it seemed to me that my studies had been limited to deepening my knowledge of music without any firm practical application. Coming as it did just then, the news of my brother's conversation with Mr. Yagi seemed like a message from heaven, and I jumped at the opportunity.

The next day, my brother took me to the Kameari plant to visit Mr. Yagi. He appeared, smiling, dressed in his work uniform. He was a handsome gentleman with a somewhat foreign countenance, resembling the French actor Charles Boyer. He must have been about 33 or 34 years old.

After introducing us to each other, my brother Toshio went back to his work in the factory. I sat down with Mr. Yagi in the reception room. The view outside the window seemed incredibly lovely, with cotton roses in full bloom in several parts of the garden. I had expected to find a noisy, greasy atmosphere, consistent with my concept of a factory. Instead, before my eyes stretched a scene of almost heavenly beauty. On that day, the color of the sky was a breathtakingly beautiful, clear blue.

"What a beautiful garden!" I exclaimed.

"Thank you," he replied, "but it's nothing special, really. Now then, we are thinking of starting several cultural activities..."

With those words, he began to speak openly about his plans and wishes, as if addressing a lifelong friend. As he spoke, his eyes radiated a clear strength, attesting to his extraordinary enthusiasm for improving the factory's cultural and employee well-being activities. As I listened, I felt as if I had already become a member of his team. That day, Mr. Yagi asked me to sing a couple of songs, and that turned out to be my entrance examination. Two or three days later, I began working at the plant.

When I began working there, however, I saw almost no sign of the plans for cultural activities that had figured so prominently in my interview with Mr. Yagi. Nor could I sense the beauty I had seen amongst the blooming flowers outside the reception room. Instead, what met my eyes and ears were the vast enclosure of the factory, filled with the noise of machinery coming from many grimy buildings, and the coarse language of the machine operators who worked hard all day to put food on their tables.

All of this confirmed my pre-conceived notions of a factory. For the management, the primary aim was to raise production levels. For the machine operators, the aim was to earn the highest possible wage. Cultural pursuits were not at all recognized as essential here.

I was employed in the Personnel Department, and my main job was to teach music, but this came about because of plans that were dear to the heart of Mr. Yagi. To my other superiors, I was just another employee who had joined the department. I began my first day in the factory's cultural activities program by helping to make posters announcing a forthcoming film.

At this plant, our main activity in looking after the workers' well-being was to distribute daily commodities. The only cultural activities that took place were the films that were shown from time to time. Making posters, preparing lists of names for the distribution of supplies, aiding the sports team and attending athletic meets—such were my initial responsibilities.

When I had begun to get accustomed to the factory atmosphere, my real work finally began: I was able to organize a chorus of female clerks who resided in the dormitory of the plant. This was followed by the formation of a youth choir, comprised of female students from the factory school, and still another choir whose members were female machine operators.

During the lunch breaks, I began to broadcast light popular and classical music and easy listening classical records together with commentaries, hoping to heal the fatigue of the workers and to nourish their spirits. Occasionally, I also staged amateur singing contests for their entertainment. In addition to these, I organized concerts of recorded music to be listened to at the close of the day.

Bit by bit, I began to extend my efforts into the literary arts, creating *tanka* and *haiku* clubs and a group that met to improve their composition and writing style. I also started a theater group. During this period, a factory newspaper began to be published, and all of a sudden, a current of human warmth began to flow through the factory.

These activities also gave us a chance to associate with other cultural groups and meet famous poets and writers. Among them were the poets Kōtaru Takamura, whose pure and simple personality was enriched with a high poetic spirit, and Teruyo Takeuchi, whose love for young people seemed to overflow from her heart. These two poets impressed me deeply. I especially remember the comment made by that noble soul, the poet Takamura:

"There are never enough words, are there!"

Those words echoed in my mind long after I heard them. It astonished me, as young person, to know that such a great poet would lament the scarcity of words available for expressing his poetic sentiments. From then on, I began to think that I must make each of my words lively and meaningful, not only in poetry but also in daily life. I continued to work with all my heart, and slowly, the workers in the plant began to soften their tough exteriors.

Gradually, this change in their attitudes brought about good results in productivity. My first, intuitive sense that this was the right place for me to work had been correct. My employment at the plant had allowed me to gain a close understanding of the daily feelings of both workers and management. I pledged to myself that I would make a sincere effort to brighten the lives of the workers, and I worked very hard at it.

In the meantime, the conflict between China and Japan had escalated into what was called the Greater East Asian War. The whole of Japan united to face this national crisis. All the factories had to increase their production even more. It was a desperate struggle, having the powerful combined forces of the United States and the British Empire as our adversaries. But my heart was filled with a belief in our certain victory, and the thought of defeat never crossed my mind. I wholly believed this was a sacred struggle, fought for God.

At that time, I had not yet experienced my spiritual awakening, and was lucky enough to be an ordinary twenty-five year old person, without any special psychic perceptions. If I had had the ability to see the future, as I have now, it would have caused me great agony, for I loved Japan and believed in it wholeheartedly. I felt an enormously profound affection for all Japanese people.

Looking back on it now, it seems that there was a divine purpose in my not going to war. It seems that I was perhaps being taught and prepared so that I could serve during the confused period that might follow.

With the outbreak of the 'Great East Asian War,' music to console and amuse the workers ceased and was replaced by military marches and songs to encourage and invigorate them. Our literary movement, too, took on a militaristic character.

Each morning at six o'clock, I would come to my office and broadcast a martial air to welcome the employees. Through the microphone, I would read them poems of military inspiration. Day and night, I did whatever I could to strengthen the workers' morale.

The plant executives were also very interested in strengthening worker morale, and they began to ascribe greater importance to my work. However, I feared that, in learning only military songs, the workers might lose touch with the deeper feelings and emotions in their hearts. By that time, though, it had become critically important that attention be focused on encouraging a militaristic spirit rather than deep lyrical feelings.

The roar of the machines was no longer treated as noise, but as a symphony celebrating our assured triumph. The workers who struggled, shirtless, before the smelting furnace, were seen as saviors of the world. All thirty thousand workers were considered heroes marching along the road to victory.

I would cry with emotion at the news of our soldiers' victories, my heart bursting with gratitude to the souls of those who had fallen in battle. My eyes filled with tears at the sight of the young boys and girls who had been employed to fill in for a decreased labor force. I earnestly prayed for and believed in Japan's victory.

Around this time, Mr. Yagi, who had been instrumental in securing my employment, was transferred to a new post as manager of the labor division of another plant, leaving his cultural innovations half-buried in the war effort. This greatly increased my workload, but I felt no fatigue.

By that time, I had completely overcome the weak constitution that I had had as a boy. I had given up my dependence on medical care at the age of about sixteen, and since that time the infirmity of my boyhood, which had been so severe that I was often referred to as "the expensive son of Goi who eats up his parents' income on medicine," had vanished.

During those youthful years, I always spent summer vacations in my father's hometown in Echigo, at the foot of the mountains. I loved to visit the temple located in the heart of those mountains. There, I would sit quietly for several hours a day. This did not arise from any conscious desire to reach a spiritual awakening, but rather from a wish to release myself from my physical infirmities. However, with the passage of time—from exactly which point, I couldn't say—my visits gradually turned into a spiritual quest aimed at uplifting myself to a state similar to *Kuu*,[6] or oneness with the essential spirit of the universe.

During this period, I would read the Holy Bible and, at times, the sutras which contained the great teachings of Buddha. In addition, I was an avid reader of the works of Mushanokoji Saneatsu,[7] and I also admired Leo Tolstoy. At about twenty-three or twenty-four years of age, I began to develop my own views on the relationship between human beings and God, although those views underwent a complete change after the war ended.

My way of meditating did not lead me to any noticeable state of spiritual illumination, but it did have the striking effect of curtailing my tendency toward illness. This was due, first of all, to my having resolved to free myself of my dependence on doctors. Secondly, the breathing exercises I had learned in my vocal studies seemed to have naturally adapted themselves to a spiritual, yoga-like method of breathing. Also, I think that the enlightened spirits of my ancestors, who resided in that mountain in my native land, must have exerted a very positive influence.

At the time I began working at Hitachi, my view on God was that God had created the world of nature and human beings, and that was all. I therefore concluded that, having been created, it was up to us human beings to fully employ the abilities we had been born with. It never once occurred to me that God would act upon human beings as an external force, to assist us in what we were doing.

It goes without saying that the existence of souls and spirits after death was a subject which never entered my head. Rather, I meditated upon the absolute purity of God as a means of purifying myself, and on the omnipotence of God as a means of encouraging myself, but I never thought of God as a being who would use external power to assist or uplift me.

My sole reliance was on my own integrity, or sense of justice, and if ever the slightest shadow was cast on it, my spirit felt severely weakened. Without a feeling of integrity, I could not take even a single step. And so, to heighten my integrity, I would pray earnestly to God. However, because I was so preoccupied with maintaining my own integrity, I found it nearly impossible to pardon dishonesty in others.

To me, integrity meant loving one's country and all people. With this in mind, I dedicated myself to the cultural program at the factory and, to increase production, I poured all my energy into raising the workers' morale.

The war grew more and more violent and, one after another, the factory workers were called away from the factory to the battlefields. Because of the shortage of workers, our workday was extended, to the point where everyone began to show signs of fatigue from overwork.

From all over Japan, boys and girls who had just graduated from elementary school came streaming into the factory to help increase production during this period. It was a touching sight to see those young girls, with their bobbed hair and their big eyes shining innocently, toiling eagerly at the foundry to form molds, or at the grindery, polishing tools.

At my request, the plant director made me responsible for the protection and care of those boys and girls, who had been recruited from all over the country. I would walk around their work areas and look after them. My aim was to protect the innocence of these young people, who worked amidst the sometimes raucous behavior of the other factory workers.

In the beginning, this duty was seen by the plant officials as unnecessary, and I was often shunned or disregarded. But gradually, young workers experiencing homesickness began demonstrating their desire to go home. As these outbursts grew more frequent, the plant executives asked me to talk with the young people and persuade them to change their minds and stay. In this way, my role suddenly became noticeable.

At the age of fourteen or fifteen, the homesick youths could not be convinced by either logic or force. Former factory workers who had been promoted to official positions had been unsuccessful in subduing these demonstrations. Persuasive words, threats, and violent admonitions only fueled their rebelliousness. The only effective influence was an outpouring of love and affection. Only someone with a loving manner could alter their heightened emotions. Only an emanation of parental, brotherly, and sisterly love could induce them to give up their wish to return home. Becoming sometimes their father or mother, sometimes their brother, sister, or friend, I comforted the children's hearts and kept them from abandoning the production plan that would help defend our country.

In this way, the plant was able to operate at full capacity, and everyone worked hard to raise production. Reports of the war, however, had begun to cast a dark shadow over Japan, and gradually, we experienced catastrophic air raids one after another.

After the first air raid, I was put in charge of broadcasting air raid protection and other plant-related instructions, and worked with the Director as a member of the plant's Central Protection Committee. With my vocal training, my pronunciation was the most articulate, and I could broadcast the instructions clearly and accurately. I would repeat the plant director's exact words the moment he had uttered them.

These broadcasts were highly appreciated. Even in a war report or an air raid alarm, I could intuitively anticipate the announcer's words before he had spoken them. Before his message had ended, I was repeating the news to everyone at the factory. Looking back on it with my current understanding, I can see that this capability of mine was a sort of psychic ability, but at the time I never thought it was anything like that. I simply thought that my mind worked quickly.

During my late teens and early twenties I had met two or three women who were mediums, but at that time, I was not ready to recognize such phenomena as psychic perceptions or the existence of souls after death. To me, a psychic telling gloomy stories to enchanted listeners was the height of the ridiculous. To begin with, those psychics and mediums struck me as having a dark and coarse air about them. Furthermore, I believed that the only absolute existence was God, and I did not wish to entertain the thought of there being various kinds of ethereal beings or creatures existing in some intangible world. And so I remained one-sidedly convinced that there could be no such thing as a spiritual power or ability issuing from another world.

Likewise, to my way of thinking, the eternal life of which Tolstoy had spoken was a matter of a person's thoughts or work being transmitted to the next generation. I was not able to attain the idea that an individual life itself would continue to exist after death. Hence, I felt that, since death was the end of everything, it was all the more important for us to live from day to day in a way that would bring us no regrets. This brought me to the conclusion that people capable of living to their utmost, with no cause for regret, would be able to reach a state of freedom from the fear of death.

My rapid, accurate broadcasts in the factory gave people a feeling of great calm and security. After a while, relaying the radio bulletins and the Protection Committee instructions turned into such an endless round of activity that my workday held no distinction between day and night.

Saipan fell, Iwo Jima was taken, and the enemy was advancing on Okinawa. Still, most Japanese people did not consider the possibility of defeat. "Soon the divine wind will come, soon the divine wind will come," seemed to be the thought in everyone's mind, as if the sacred wind that aided Japan's victory in the attacks of Genkō[8] would again come to our rescue. But Okinawa fell into enemy hands, and the bombings reached their highest pitch.

We began to sleep at the plant, and we worked ceaselessly. Because an air raid might come at any time, no one slept soundly. It seemed to me that the job I was doing could be done by anyone, but that was not the case. Even when there was a substitute, his speed and accuracy were too different from mine. This had a negative impact on the workers' morale, creating an atmosphere of insecurity throughout the plant.

Since everyone in the factory wished it, I stayed on

duty in the broadcasting room twenty-four hours a day. Gazing at the microphone, I felt not the least bit tired, and my cheerful mood seemed impossible to shatter. I felt that, were I to perish in a bomb attack, I would die happy, for I was focusing all my strength on working for the good of the country, and that feeling seemed to brighten my spirits. I thought only of doing my ut-most, and left the rest to Providence.

Meanwhile, the tide of the war was increasingly turning against us. Due to the incessant bombings, production was dropping further and further. Japan had reached, we thought, the final stage in the war, and we were ready to join in a decisive battle for our national territory. That Japan had been defeated—that such a tragedy had become reality—did not fully envelop me until the very last day, when I heard the Emperor's broadcast.

For me, my homeland—Japan—was an absolute existence, and its Emperor a manifestation of God. When this divine being broadcast his message of Japan's defeat, proclaiming the war to be over, it pained my heart and caused me to weep bitterly.

"...this 15th day of August, 1945. Thus ends the Emperor's broadcast." With these words I switched off the equipment. The director and I embraced one another and continued to weep. That night, I composed the following poem:

Majestic, venerable words,
drenched with sorrow,
spoken by the Emperor,
penetrating the hearts
of a hundred million patriots.
Through his voice,
the mournful divine sentiment draws near.
Crying out in a voice
of fathomless anguish,
we rail in vain against heaven and earth
at the reality of this defeat:
There is no place to hide one's own shadow.
Three thousand years of history
fell to the earth in an instant,
a nostalgic memory from a distant time.
The Emperor bestows divine love
on this wounded and confused people.
There is nothing further to be done.
We were an arrogant people;
We tried to dominate other countries;
We distanced ourselves from our allies;
We did not cultivate respect.
We distressed our divine Emperor
and, inevitably, the country was defeated.
Oh, I have no further words to say.
Following the will of the Emperor,
May the one hundred million souls of this country
do their penance and dwell in a renewed homeland.

After I had wept all the tears that streamed from

my grieving heart, I was surprised to find new strength springing forth from deep within me. That night, I wrote the following lines, strongly affirming that we had lost the war because we were meant to lose it. I was ready to watch the great changes that would take place in this country from that day forth.

> Victory and defeat do not concern me.
> My spirit is purifying itself
> to serve the world.
> It is time to cast off our old shells,
> shoulder the hardships,
> and rebuild a new Land.

Such was the feeling that arose in my heart.

Seeking the Divine Self

This defeat, the first in Japan's history, threw the people's minds into utter confusion. As the U.S. Army began entering each region, the terrified citizens spread rumors of various types. For example, they said that the women would be raped, and that the men would be enslaved and forced to work.

In the factory, where all production had ceased, there was a strange atmosphere—a mixture of relief over the end of the air raids which had gone on daily during the war, and a budding anxiety over the future. This made the workers unusually talkative. Had they not been able to talk things over with each other, they might have felt even more insecure about what the future would bring.

All of a sudden, I reached a decision to leave the plant. I intuitively felt that my role there had come to an end, and that my life would take a sudden turn in an unexpected direction. I felt that my real life was just beginning and, despite having no prospects for the future, I felt a new strength arising from deep in my heart.

At the factory, an appeal went out for people who knew some English. The director suggested that I start working as an interpreter, but I excused myself, saying that my English was not good enough. Instead, I told him that I wished to resign from my job at the factory as soon as things were put in order.

Before I could resign, the main task at hand was to send the young factory workers, who had come from various regions of the country, back to their hometowns. This was primarily the responsibility of the Personnel Department, but as a member of the Protection Committee, I could not just stand idly by and leave all the work up to others. Besides, the affection that I felt for each of those young people made me want to see them returned to their families as quickly as possible.

I urged the Personnel Department to work on this as quickly as they could. I also tried hard to obtain train tickets for their various destinations. At that time, it was difficult to get train tickets in large quantities, but thanks to everyone's efforts we were able to make the necessary arrangements for sending the children back to their homes sooner than we had expected.

It was decided that one official would accompany each group travelling to their native province, and I decided, of my own volition, to accompany the group going to Miyazaki Prefecture. The children were always telling me proudly about their native regions, and of these, the stories of Miyazaki had intrigued me the most. Perhaps this was because the Hyūga region in Miyazaki was reputed to be the place where, in ancient times, heavenly descendents had come down to Earth. I had been wishing to go to Hyūga with these children someday after the war ended, which to me, of course, had meant after Japan's victory.

Hyūga was where the new utopian community of Mushanokoji Saneatsu, called 'new village,' was located, and since I was very interested in the new village, I had been hoping to be able to go there. However, the day before our departure for Hyūga, fate stepped in and prevented my trip from happening. It seemed that my soul was destined to gain further experiences in post-war Tokyo instead.

Nearly six months before the war's end, I had suffered a complication with my kidneys, but because the country was in a state of emergency and because it was extremely important to maintain a calm and safe atmosphere at the factory, it didn't occur to me to take time off and rest. The factory physician had warned me that if I continued at that pace, diabetes symptoms would emerge within a week, and my condition would become aggravated and difficult to cure. He insisted that I obtain permission to take some time off to rest. I appreciated his concern, but did not ask for a single day off. I was determined to go on working even if it meant that I would die in the process.

During that period, I had borrowed a book from a Ms. Koda, who worked as a clerk in the Personnel Department. It had a title like *Tomorrow's Medicine*, and was written by Mokichi Okada, founder of a new spiritual entity which is now known as *sekai meshiya kyō* (世界救世教). His method was then called a 'purification method,' and Misao Koda, the mother of the young woman who had lent me the book, was kind enough to apply this treatment to me.

According to Mokichi Okada's theory, all human illnesses occur as manifestations of a purification process by which toxic elements are eliminated from the body. Some of these toxins are said to arise from the unharmonious thoughts and actions (karma) of one's ancestors, and others are the manifestations of karma from the person's own previous lifetimes. All these poisonous elements are dissipated through fevers, and the motive power comes from the natural healing power that all human beings have. Though the body may suffer the discomfort of a fever, this is merely a means for eliminating toxins and is not harmful in any way; it occurs naturally in the process of purifying the human body.

The theory explains that if one takes an excess of medicines, it will suppress the fever, causing the toxins to remain in the body instead of being released. Furthermore, additional toxins, contained in the medicines themselves, are introduced within the body.

Thus, as the variety of medications increase, poisonous elements in the human body also increase. Diseases become difficult to eliminate, and additional, more serious illnesses begin to appear. All of this happens because we resist the processes of nature. It is recommended that, rather than resist these processes, we leave everything to our natural curative power.

The book also explains that from the palms of the hands there radiates a divine light, described as 'spiritual rays.' When we place our palms over the kidneys, the purifying center of the human body, and then on each of the places to be cured, the purification process is promoted, the pain lessens, and healing occurs naturally.

I agreed wholeheartedly with this theory, based on my past experiences, through which I had eventually overcome my fragile constitution by throwing out my medicines, giving up on doctors, and entrusting myself wholly to my natural healing power.

Also, the theory that the toxins contained in medicines actually cause disease, and that fevers occur in order to release those substances, challenged the supposition that fevers should be avoided. The author's firm, resolute tone was very pleasing to me. I judged him to be a wise person, and wished to know more about him.

Since I saw no reason to dispute the existence of spiritual rays emanating from the palms of the hands, I underwent two or three days of *shiatsu* treatment,[9] performed with great care by the elder Ms. Koda. As these treatments progressed, my kidney complications gradually disappeared. At the time, however, I did not pay much attention to this, because I was far too busy to think about it. This was about the time when the war ended and Japan surrendered.

The day before I was to leave for Hyūga, the pain in my kidneys, which I had completely forgotten about, suddenly recurred. My legs felt so heavy that I could scarcely move them. When I finally got to the factory, it was clear to everyone that I was too exhausted to make a long trip. So, in the end, I had to give up on travelling to Miyazaki.

The children said goodbye to me in the factory, and they seemed very disappointed that I was not going with them. The symptoms intensified, and from that day on I stayed in bed. Since I did not visit a doctor, I do not know, even to this day, what my illness was. For several days, I sustained a fever of 40 degrees (about 104 degrees Fahrenheit). My breathing was labored and my whole body ached, from the top of my head to the tips of my toes. It was clear to everyone at home (my mother, my brother, and his wife) that this was not simply a complication with my kidneys. My family insisted on calling a doctor, but in the halting phrases I was able to speak, I managed to stop them from doing so. I appreciated my family's love and concern, but I believed beyond the shadow of a doubt that my own vital force would cure me of this illness. Because of this belief, I felt no fear.

In spite of being bedridden for nearly a week and unable to take anything except water due to the high fever, the thought of dying never crossed my mind. From somewhere deep within me, an unshakable assurance welled up that my return to good health was only a matter of time.

I imagine that the accumulation of tension and physical fatigue, caused by overwork during the war, was being released all at once and manifesting itself in the form of pneumonia, brain and kidney inflammation, and other symptoms, all occurring simultaneously. When the fatigue was eliminated, the illness would certainly disappear. Amidst my labored breathing, I seemed to be observing myself being born anew, and I wholly believed that after all my fatigue had gone, I would emerge as a new person.

About ten days later, I had recovered completely. From the day I got out of bed, my body, which had borne such a high fever day after day, never again suffered pain or showed any marked weakness.

"It was the absence of fear that prevented my body from weakening," I told myself. "Fear is the enemy of everything. A bright, positive, spirit triumphs over all." Recalling these words, which I had once heard someone say, the thought flashed into my mind that the way to revitalize postwar Japan might be found through a reorientation of the mind and spirit.

Shortly after this experience, I resigned from my job at Hitachi. I gathered some friends together and formed a musical group, wishing to give a spark of hope to the confused people of Japan. But this turned out to be a resounding failure.

I had intended for my group to play classical music. However, people now seemed to prefer a type of jazz which had come with the stationing of U.S. troops. As a result, our group found itself unable to earn enough to be financially independent by playing classical music alone. Even so, my conscience would not allow me to turn to jazz for purely financial reasons. Considering the times we were living in, my mother thought my decision rather extravagant. But since I had quit my job in such a resolute manner, she did not try to dissuade me. She knew very well that I could be very unyielding once my mind was made up.

From that day on, and for quite some time, we had to live by selling off our belongings. There were three in our household, including my brother, who had just returned from the war, my mother, and me. We all lived at the home of my older brother and his wife, but my mother's firm character made her very strict about our not interfering in the couple's lives. With this thought always in mind, she managed to keep our household separate from theirs.

Our musical instruments, phonograph, and records were all sold. Amidst the steadily disappearing furnishings of the house, I searched and yearned for a new world.

One of the things that I pursued was Mokichi Okada's treatment method involving spiritual rays. According to Ms. Koda, Mr. Okada called his treatment a 'spiritual science,' and not a religion. Even so, I clearly sensed a religious atmosphere behind it. Mr. Okada occupied the position of founder, and sent his top-level instructors to various places. Those instructors, in turn, had subordinate instructors, and those subordinates had students of their own. In this way, Mr. Okada's influence had already attained considerable proportions.

Accompanied by Ms. Koda, I visited a treatment center under the charge of one of the top-level instructors, a man named Mr. Y. Just by looking at Mr. Y, one could see that he was a wonderful, warmhearted person. As he proceeded with the treatment, he talked about a variety of things. His comments dealt mostly with the actual contents of Mr. Okada's book, but the topic of the spiritual world also arose.

Handing me a nearby book, which I estimated to contain about 200 pages, he said, "If this book were understood, all other theories would have no importance." This book had also been written by Mr. Okada, and it dealt with topics such as speaking with departed souls and the effects produced by possessing spirits. Upon reading it, I got an uncomfortable impression similar to the embarrassed feeling one gets in looking at a work of poor quality fiction—that it was indecorous and inartistic. Although I had been impressed by Mr. Okada's previous book, *Tomorrow's Medicine*, I felt indifferent toward this one. I wondered why Mr. Y had attached such importance to this work, and why he had recommended it to me.

I had been easily convinced by the message in *Tomorrow's Medicine*, that powerful spiritual rays of light radiating from the palms of the hands could influence one's well-being. I also understood that human disease was caused by toxic substances and that fever occurs in order to dissolve these substances and eliminate them from the body. All this was indisputably true as far as I was concerned. Natural healing power was something I knew about very well because of my own past experiences. I felt reassured by Mr. Okada's assertion that relying too much on doctors and medicines would weaken the healing power within us.

Despite my admiration for Mr. Okada's firm statements regarding the above, his second book evoked no such feelings in me. Seeing that I was not so impressed with it, Mr. Y said, smiling, "This book is one that takes time to understand. Gradually, I think you may form a higher opinion of it." I felt more attracted to Mr. Y's personality than to the book. He seemed to me a truly good person, one of rare human warmth.

From that day on, I called on Mr. Y occasionally, and listened to him talk about Mr. Okada's ideas and his life, and about the method of healing people with spiritual rays.

Around this time, I read another book—one that had caught my attention when visiting a musician friend of mine, Mr. M. It was entitled *Hyaku Ji Nyoi*,[10] by Masaharu Taniguchi.[11] I read the book in a single sitting and felt overcome with profound emotion. It was as if my eyes had suddenly been opened. I had already known of Masaharu Taniguchi's importance for some time through his work *Kanro no Hōu* (The Holy Sutra). Someone had shown it to me almost ten years before, but I recall that I had not read it seriously.

After I finished reading *Hyaku Ji Nyoi*, I was eager to read other books like it. With that thought in mind, I began, at Ms. Koda's home, to practice the healing method involving spiritual rays that had been recommended to me by Mr. Y. From the depths of my heart, I yearned to do something useful for humanity and for the world. I was willing to do anything if it would be helpful to others. I had no intention of amusing myself by toying with theories. I was only interested in practice.

Among the poems I wrote during this period were these two:

If my wish meets Your Will,
Let my life be joined in Your Work
To uplift Japan from its defeat.

My heart is burning with the wish
To become a thread
Joining the earth with the sky.

As the above poems express, I earnestly wished to devote my life entirely to my country and to humanity. I did not have any preference as to the type of work, but strongly wished to fulfill my mission for the human world.

Using Ms. Koda's house as a base, I traveled around

doing healing work. Placing my palms above the afflicted person and vibrating them, or pressing the patient's body with my fingers as in *shiatsu*, brought considerably good results. The people who had been healed were pleased and offered me little packages containing money, but I would always refuse them and rush away. Since I had begun to feel that this work had a divine purpose, I strongly felt that I should not take any payment for it. I felt that only through voluntary work, freely given, could one live a noble life. Guided by this ideal, I kept up my work. Every time a person was cured, my joy would transport me to a state of paradise. A simple "Thank you" was enough to satisfy me completely.

Meanwhile, in contrast to my own high spirits, the dwindling condition of my mother's purse intensified her feelings of discontent:

"I'm not saying that it's right to insist upon payment or set a price for every service, but what is the harm in accepting what people offer as a token of their appreciation?" My mother did not object to my spiritual way of life, but she often expressed dissatisfaction with the willful attitude of this son of hers, who looked upon money as if it were an enemy. And, as she found it increasingly difficult to raise money for groceries by selling our belongings, her tone became more serious. I listened to her lectures as though she were talking to someone else, and continued in the same way as before. But when someone offered me vegetables or fish, I began to accept them without objection and bring them home.

While continuing to practice my healing method, I avidly read many spiritual and philosophical books. Among them were more books by Dr. Masaharu Taniguchi, which my friend A had loaned me—the *Seimei no Jisso* (生命の實相—Truth of Life) series. This collection consisted of twenty volumes, which I read through at one stretch. Through them, I became distinctly aware that other worlds existed which were unknown to me, and that the physical body was merely one manifestation of the human existence.

This knowledge had been absorbed from books and not through experience, but I had the feeling that I understood it clearly and had already experienced all of it.

Those two great human beings—Mokichi Okada and Masaharu Taniguchi—appeared in my life at the same time, while I was striving for rebirth after Japan's defeat in the war.

Mokichi Okada had unshakable confidence in his assertions, but composed only straightforward prose passages. Masaharu Taniguchi, on the other hand, captivated his readers with his delicate, detailed writings. Both of these people—giant, contrasting personalities (or so I thought at that time)—wrote about the existence of the spiritual world and tried to demonstrate the unending life of the individual soul. The evidence provided in their books easily transformed me into a proponent of the principle that spirits and souls live on after the death of the physical body.

Perhaps it was my openness, or my natural temperament, that enabled me to change. In any case, these books were the spark that turned me toward my study of the spiritual and subconscious worlds, and launched my relentless pursuit of the inner divine self.

One day in late spring, I visited Mr. Mokichi Okada in Atami, Shizuoka Prefecture, accompanied by Mr. Y. Mr. Okada did not receive visitors indiscriminately—he saw only people who had attended the lectures given by his high-level instructors, and only when they were brought to him by those instructors.

Entering his spacious residence, which we reached after walking up several inclines, we found many people already there. Each one presented a donation prepared ahead of time. Since Ms. Koda had told me about this before we went, I had put some money from my nearly empty wallet into an envelope and now placed it on a stand in front of the receptionist. There were several waiting areas where groups of people were eating their lunches or talking with each other.

Their conversations, which I unintentionally overheard, gave me the odd impression that they were not taking place in this world. Just like the stories about ghosts told by the female mediums I had met in my twenties, these conversations dealt with monsters which were never heard or seen, as well as long-nosed goblins, and foxes and snakes that possessed people. The people were boasting that their 'light' (spiritual ray healing) had exorcised and subdued these monsters, and that the afflicted people had been cured. At least these people were more believable than the mediums, as they did not have the shadowy aura of the occult about them. Regardless of whether their stories were true or not, I felt uncomfortable and embarrassed and did not feel at all like talking or associating with them. I had the impression that the path that I was seeking existed in a world far removed from theirs.

Mr. Y closed his eyes, wiped both his cheeks, and passed his hands over his face. He seemed truly relaxed and at ease. This man was different from the rest of the group—he seemed to live in his own world.

The time came at last when we could see Mr. Okada. The people began gathering in the hall where Mr. Okada, seated at a desk, was consecrating a newly made image of Buddha. When all the people had settled down and become quiet, they all bowed together respectfully, as if at a signal. Bowing like the others, I was the first to raise my head and was surprised to see that no one else had done so. I could not help but look in Mr. Okada's direction, and saw the receptionist reverently place the stand of gifts before him. Mr. Okada fingered the envelopes, turning them over as if examining them, and nodded.

He was a man of slight stature, with graying hair, and looked to me more like a skilled artisan than a spiritual leader or life-guide. I was rather surprised by his appearance, because I had come in search of an image resembling Christ or Buddha.

All around me people began to stir, as I listened absent-mindedly. They had raised their heads and begun to report on the results of their healing practices and their activities to spread Mr. Okada's teachings. They gave their reports one after another, and many of them told stories of healings similar to the ones I had heard in the waiting room.

The meeting was interesting, for I had never attended such a gathering before, but I could not, even for a moment, sense an atmosphere of sanctity or spiritual awe.

Mr. Okada's lecture followed the reports, and then there were questions and answers between him and his top-level instructors. However, there was not enough inspirational content to enrapture my soul. Mr. Okada seemed to be a person of intuitively guided action rather than one geared to study or discussion. Still, his ideas were wide-ranging, and I was attracted by his calm yet confident way of speaking and his large-scale, universal outlook. I think it was because I had been harboring strong objections to the Japanese people's self-abasing attitude after our country's defeat.

Seeing him that one time, I got the feeling that Mr. Okada was a combination of politician, businessman, and entrepreneur, rather than a spiritually-oriented figure. His intuitive quality may have been what made people regard him as a spiritual leader.

My visit there gave me hope for all Japanese people, as I realized that here was an enterprising person who unhesitatingly put his ideas into practice with a firm sense of conviction, even in this defeated nation. Here was a person of great confidence who did not fear the victorious English and Americans, and who ignored the Russians. His example enabled me to embrace new hope for the Japanese people. However, the saintly image of a true leader for Japan, which I had been looking for in him, faded like a dream.

The main objective of my visit had not been fulfilled, but hearing people discuss their experiences in healing the afflicted with spiritual rays strengthened my confidence, reinforced my own experience, and gave me the assurance that I too could help to heal the afflicted. It was after this that I began, in all earnest, to practice healing treatments on the ill.

All of Mr. Okada's adherents wore a paper amulet next

to their skin on which his calligraphy, *kōmyō* (光明—light) was written. They believed that divine light, working through the amulet, would heal those who were ill. My faith in the amulet became uncertain after having seen him, because my image of him as a saint had been somewhat altered. Instead, I was becoming more confident that I could heal people directly with my own inner power, and I felt sure that the secret to healing people lay in selfless and genuine love.

Because of this, I found myself increasingly reluctant to accept material rewards. If money was offered as a remuneration, I turned red with embarrassment and felt like running away. Nevertheless, enough money to cover my transportation expenses was either delivered to my mother or given through Ms. Koda.

Although I was growing materially poorer day by day, my heart was bright and clear. Looking up at the sky, as though being absorbed into it, I continued calling to the divine presence in my mind, and prayed continuously: "Please use my life for your work. Please show me my true, divinely-given purpose in this world as soon as possible."

I loved the sky. I could not help but love it. Of course, I liked the blue sky infinitely, but even on a cloudy or rainy day, it was very pleasant to look up at the sky. Since childhood, I had firmly retained the idea that I had once dwelt in a heavenly world. In my poem *"Kogarashi"* (Cold Winter Wind), written earlier in my life, there often appeared phrases such as "I who used to be a heavenly child" or "After finishing one more task, I shall take a rest in the moon." In another poem called "Rain," there is the phrase: "I came out of a wish to spread heaven's mercies on earth."

Thus, I would always think about the relationship between heaven and earth, and lived with my mind turned toward the sky. Despite living in Asakusa, a district in Tokyo where small houses stood close together, and which was crowded with shops and pedestrians, I would forget everything and become absorbed in the beauty of the sky. There was no special reason for this; I simply loved the sky.

One day, I went to see a new patient who lived in a farmhouse by the Naka River, on the side which was closer to Chiba Prefecture. The second son of the family, about twenty years old, was suffering from peritoneal tuberculosis. He was already in a grave state, to the extent that pus was oozing out ceaselessly and the doctor had already given up hope on him. His family had heard of me and come to me in desperation, asking me to see him. As most of my patients had recovered their health wonderfully, I was not anxious about his condition, and acceded to their request without hesitation.

I walked all the way to the house, not even thinking of the young man or his symptoms, but just reflecting on the existence of divine love and calling to God in my heart. Confidently, I strode along, my face turned toward the blue summer sky. Along the riverbank, the young leaves of the cherry trees were shining beautifully in the sun. Ripples from the waves glittered on the river's surface.

Everything around me—the rustling of the leaves and the sparkling puddles of water—appeared so beautiful. While absorbed in the beauty of nature and thinking how breathtakingly lovely it was, I also heard an aching voice from somewhere within my heart, crying, "I cannot allow myself to wholly melt into this beauty until illness, affliction, poverty, and hardship have been erased from the world." I felt as if I were responsible for removing them.

As if in response to that emerging voice, I repeated my habitual, heartfelt thought—"God, please use my life for your work"—and kept on walking. When I arrived at the landing dock of the ferry to cross the river, and was about to go down to the bank, a voice reverberated through my mind like thunder: "God has received your life. Are you ready?"

The voice came from neither my head nor my heart, but was a meaningful resonance emanating from heaven. It was most definitely a voice, and it spoke words. However, it was different from the human-sounding spiritual voices that I was to hear later, from morning till night each day. "Yes!" I replied, without a moment's hesitation.

From that instant, my whole being was given to the divine will. The personal 'self' of Masahisa Goi ceased to exist. However, it would take a fair amount of time before the reality of this would become apparent on the surface.

For a while, I stood still on the riverbank, my eyes closed, unable to think anything. After some time had passed, I opened my eyes, as if awakening from a dream. The sun was shining brilliantly, and the birds' singing was pleasant to my ears. Massaging away the stiffness of my momentary tension, I headed toward the ferry.

"My life already belongs to heaven," I thought. "This physical body of mine exists here, running through heaven and earth." My heart felt absolutely clear, and I had no doubts about the heavenly voice.

When I arrived at the patient's house, his family received me with an air of great anticipation. As I went and sat by his bedside, his mother began to sadly describe his symptoms to me. The patient turned his ghastly face toward us, then immediately closed his eyes again.

"You see...this is how he is," his mother said, using a pair of wooden chopsticks to apprehensively lift the cotton swab that covered his navel. With every breath the patient took, his navel exuded a greenish fluid, alternating in color and thickness as he inhaled and exhaled. Immediately,

I began the healing treatment, with the feeling that doctors could do nothing more for him. The patient kept his eyes closed, in dead silence. His expression seemed to say, "Why go to all this trouble if I won't recover anyway?" He seemed to have totally given up.

As I placed my hand above his navel area, the fluid started to fly out even more profusely. "The poisons are being discharged," I thought to myself. "When they disappear completely, he will recover." Indeed, I had no doubt of this, for I fully believed in Mr. Okada's theory.

Repeatedly, I wiped off the fluid with cotton swabs and continued the treatment. When the treatment had been completed, the patient's mother brought me some water so that I could wash my hands. "No, that's all right. His illness will not affect me," I said, refusing her offer. Although my hands were covered with the pus that had leaked through the cotton swabs, my attitude was nonchalant. Normally, common sense would have led me to wash my hands, but in this case I purposely refrained from doing so because it bothered me that the family was so worried about becoming infected. Naturally, they had been cautioned by the doctors, but I felt that if you really want to heal someone, you cannot be afraid of contagion.

Since it was just about noon, I was offered a lunch of rice balls and pickled vegetables. As I picked them up, my fingers covered with pus, and ate them delightedly, the family gazed at me in astonishment. Later, I heard from the mother that the doctors had told them: "Tuberculosis is a dreadful disease and is terribly infectious. The disease may be transferred merely by being near the patient. If your hand comes in contact with the pus, and is not thoroughly washed, the consequences are horrendous." Thus, the family's apprehensive attitude stemmed from their fear of contracting tuberculosis. This was understandable, but it was not very helpful to the patient.

Until then, the youth had kept his eyes closed in silence, but at that moment, deeply moved, he cried, "Thank you! Thank you very much!" Then he burst into a flood of tears.

Because of their fear of infection, both the doctors and the patient's family had kept their distance from him, and so he was surprised and delighted at my casual manner in treating him as a routine patient. Placing my hands on his blanket, I said to him, "Once it starts to improve, a disease is usually cured very quickly. It's important to be positive. When the poisonous substances have been discharged completely, you'll become healthier than you ever used to be. Most people are not aware of the divine healing power that exists in their bodies. Since I know of this power, I'm trying to draw it out from within you. From now on, let's work as a team. We'll get through this together, you and I."

The youth nodded several times and then said with a big smile, "Yes, I'll be brave! I'll do as you say."

"This is the first time my boy has smiled in a long time," his mother said, her features relaxing in a happy expression.

From the following day on, I went to the boy's house every day, and his condition gradually improved. At one point, when the pus had almost stopped flowing, he became able to sit up in bed and read books for almost half a day when he felt well enough.

As I continued to practice these kinds of healing treatments, my family's financial state gradually worsened. My brother, though still regaining his strength after returning from the war, could not turn down a friend's offer to work with him, selling goods at an outdoor stand. This income barely supported our family. Although I felt badly for him, I continued to energetically pursue my own divine mission. My brother understood this very well and tried not to let me worry about money. "I'll take care of the financial side," he said reassuringly, "so that you can show us the results of your great work as soon as possible."

During this period, I was seriously engaged in my search for the true human identity, while devoting my daily efforts to healing people. I subscribed to the monthly magazine called *Seicho-No-Ie*, issued by Masaharu Taniguchi's organization.[12] I also visited many mediums to find evidence of the existence of spiritual beings, and looked for books relating to psychic phenomena. The members of Seicho-No-Ie who lived nearby visited me often. Since I had a great admiration for their series of books, *The Truth of Life*, I felt an increasing interest in their monthly magazine. I sincerely wished to meet the group's founder, who I thought might well be the second coming of Christ or the messiah. Whether it was predestined or just by chance, I do not know, but it turned out that the founder was born on the same day I was, twelve hours earlier—he at sunrise and I at sunset. I felt a deep connection between us.

One Sunday, I asked my older and younger brothers to accompany me to the main headquarters of Seicho-No-Ie, located in front of the Nogi Shrine in Akasaka, Tokyo. When we entered the lecture hall on the second floor, the founder, Masaharu Taniguchi, was about to begin his lecture. Sitting on a stage about three feet above where we were seated, he looked about at the assembled listeners with a smile. As I gazed at him, knowing that he had written those great books, the *Truth of Life* series, I realized that I had unknowingly built up an idealized image of him in my mind. As his appearance did not coincide with my ideal image of how a saintly being should look, I was left feeling a bit perplexed. This feeling quickly vanished, however, upon hearing the wonderful contents of his talk and his captivating way of speaking. His broad forehead, attesting to intellectual depth, his piercing eyes, and his rich use of words, flowing from steadfast thought—all these signs of a scholarly approach contrasted with the bearing of Mr. Okada. Taniguchi Sensei[13] had a rather philosophical air about him.

Though during the war, there were frequent references to 'Japan's ultimate victory' and 'the inevitable defeat of America and Britain' in the publications of Seicho-No-Ie, I paid little attention to such passing trends. Instead, I was deeply affected by such concepts as the perfectly harmonious nature of a human being, and the idea that the original self contains no element of evil, trouble, or disease. Such were the underlying themes of Taniguchi Sensei's writings.

Therefore, during his talk that day, I found myself far more attracted by his theory that we are originally perfect and integral beings than by any comments dealing with personal benefits and advantages.

It was stated in the *Truth of Life* series that there are two types of thoughts: one vertical and the other horizontal. The concept of 'vertical thought,' which so impressed me, includes the theory that humans are, in reality, perfect beings, free from the pains of aging, illness, disease, and other forms of suffering, and that our physical body does not truly exist.

Consequently, there cannot be any pain from illness,

or any hardship from poverty. Only a confused mind believes in such illusions, for in the ultimate reality, there are no such things as physical beings or material substances. What we believe we see are just shadows of our deluded thoughts. The only truth is that nothing exists but God. Such were the principles that won my heart.

The concept of 'horizontal thought' has its roots in the Buddhist concept that all is a reflection of the mind, and in the theory of thought waves, which is presented in the study of mental science. The idea is that, since our minds work as a creative force, all situations manifest according to how we direct our thoughts. Our present hardships are the results of negative and incorrect thoughts which we have projected. Evil will manifest if we have evil thoughts, and good will manifest if we have good thoughts. If we happen to be suffering from an illness, its cause can be found in our unharmonious thoughts and actions. We are responsible for everything that happens to us, because it is all a shadow projected by our own mind.

The books continued to cite examples using these two thought principles. They were spiritual books aimed at unifying all religions, and they dealt with the studies of Buddhism, Christianity, Tenri-kyō,[14] Kurozumi-kyō,[15] mental science, psychic science, and others. Until I reached my own divine awakening later in life, I firmly believed that there could be no greater a teaching than this, nor would there ever be anyone whose understanding could surpass these principles. If anyone were to speak disparagingly about these teachings, I would think that he or she was surely mistaken. I truly felt that this was, without a doubt, a flawless doctrine.

However, it is sometimes the case that teachings that are too structured become rather difficult to follow. There are also instances where too much perfectionism is, itself, a fatal flaw. If they are properly understood by each person, the vertical and horizontal principles could indeed yield beneficial effects. On the other hand, if they are improperly understood, they could have unharmonious effects and leave terrible scars on one's soul. Later on, as I gained experience as an instructor for Seicho-No-Ie, I gradually became aware of concerns like this, and they became even more distinct after I reached my own awakening.

In any case, this realization did not come to me until much later in life. On the day when I first saw Taniguchi Sensei, I was overwhelmed with tears of gratitude after joining in the final prayer, called *shinsokan* (神想観). My brothers were not as deeply touched as I was, and remained somewhat critical, which bothered me slightly.

From that day on, I became an active member of Seicho-No-Ie. In addition to attending Taniguchi Sensei's lectures on Sundays, I visited the main headquarters each day to listen to other speakers. Each and every speaker seemed incredibly great to me. Meanwhile, I called upon my neighborhood subscribers in the hope of organizing a local branch. As a result, the Katsushika Group was formed. A senior member became the group chairperson and I took the position of vice-chair. With high spirits, I actively set out to seek new participants, and dedicated myself to spreading the group's principles of positive thinking.

At that time, I felt that I could gladly become a factotum to Taniguchi Sensei. I regarded his spiritual state as equal to that of Buddha and Christ. Furthermore, I strongly believed that the principles of Seicho-No-Ie were the only hope for the revival of the Japanese spirit, as well as for the deliverance of all human beings. Ever since my encounter with Mr. Mokichi Okada, I had jumped at every chance to meet highly respected figures that I heard good things about, as long as my funds permitted. Though superior qualities were inherent in each of them, until now I hadn't come across anyone who totally won me over.

It did not occur to me until later that my encounter with Taniguchi Sensei was with the author of the *Truth of Life* series. To me, Masaharu Taniguchi was equivalent to the books. In fact, I only had occasional glimpses of an individual called Masaharu Tani-guchi who existed separately from the books. During the time when I was a devoted adherent of Seicho-No-Ie, I never actually had a chance to meet him personally.

Indeed, the Taniguchi Sensei that I had gotten to know through the teachings in his books was wonderful, and his principles were of a remarkably high quality. Nevertheless, it would later become apparent to me that there was a gap between his actual deeds and the high ideals described in his books. Likewise, the tendencies of his students did not bear out the proposition that one's 'true image' would easily appear if the teachings were followed. This was something that I clearly reconfirmed later on. And, this may well have been what induced me to gradually drift away from Seicho-No-Ie, and to be given the task of developing a new spiritual teaching that could rectify such tendencies as over-talkativeness and exaggerated expressions, which tend to impede a person's progress toward spiritual awakening. Thus would begin the birth of a new spiritual method, and I would thereafter feel that a new way of life was taking shape in accordance with the divine will.

The fact that Taniguchi Sensei and I were born on the same day, he at sunrise and I at sunset, may very well have been symbolically meaningful in terms of this hidden divine plan.

The Divine Plan

The power of material things in this realistic world is so great, it could almost be considered absolute. However distinguished we might be in the spiritual sense, we could not survive in this world without the aid of material things. In order to continue existing on Earth, we must acquire material things, and for that we inevitably have to make some sort of physical or mental efforts.

People who find that they can support themselves solely through their dedication to some kind of spiritual aim are quite rare, and most of them have had the experience of working for material things in the past. In my case, my spiritual quest and my entire life thus far had been dedicated to a wholehearted search for truth. However, if I had gone on refusing to think about earning a living, the door to a material life would surely have closed for me.

My work was to heal the sick. I could have earned my living at it, had I not refused to accept money for this service. However, I rejected the idea of using this work as a source of income. I felt that this was sacred work and that it was wrong to accept money for it.

How, then, could I earn my living? I had no means of earning income apart from my healing work. Actually, it was not that there were no other sources; it was just that I had not tried to and in fact had no desire to look for other work. As a result, my mother and I were totally dependent on the income provided by my younger brother.

However, even that income came from a job he himself did not particularly like. Was it wrong of me, I wondered, to ignore my mother's qualms about this situation, out of a conviction that my healing work, freely given, was in keeping with the divine plan for my life? Some strong words from my mother one day set me on the path towards a solution.

One August morning, as I prepared to go out and perform my usual healing treatments, my mother called to me, "Masahisa, how long do you intend to go on like this? What you are doing is helping people, and I think that is fine. I can also see the integrity in your actions. But I think it's odd that you can't go on helping people without your younger brother's support. You will never be independent if you go on this way. You will always be reliant on your brother's kindness. If you really want to help others, first of all, you must help yourself. Don't you think it's a bit strange to try and help others while you yourself are placing a burden on someone else? If you go on doing this work, you must accept fair payment for it. Or else, get a job somewhere and help others during your free time. Up to now, I have kept quiet about it, but now you must make a definite choice."

We then agreed that if this matter were not settled by the fifth of September, I would have to leave the house. Clearly, my mother thought that it was not good for either my brother or me to go on like this, and I think she was right.

From that day on, I began looking for a job. There was no way I could be persuaded to accept money for my healing work. Instead, I decided to carry out this divinely given work during my free time.

Having made this decision, I didn't feel any particular tension about it. I shifted my mind in the direction of finding a job, but my fundamental idea was unchanged. Ever since I had heard that voice from heaven, I felt that, since I had entrusted myself completely to the divine will, God would certainly make use of my existence. With this in mind, I lived with an optimistic, free, and easy feeling.

I started studying the newspaper ads and calling on

acquaintances. I also inquired at places that had advertised work. Although I was not a victim of war, I didn't own a decent suit of clothing, or even a new shirt. All those things had already been sold off to pay for our living expenses. Wearing a freshly washed, carefully patched shirt, a pair of trousers with a big patch in the seat, and old shoes nearly flapping open, and carrying a dish of sweet potatoes in my lunchbox, I confidently set out to look for a job.

Though it was only a year after the war, people were starting to clearly feel that the future was open to everyone, and that each individual could move ahead on his or her own path. Those with business acumen had already found jobs in new services or businesses. The cautious, prudent ones had stayed with their former companies. Established companies did not need new employees, and although new companies were looking for technicians and workers experienced in sales and promotion, they rarely needed a cultural director like me.

"I'll do any kind of work," I would say, but the employers rejected me without further explanation. Despite being turned down time and again, I continued my job hunt day after day. "I wonder where the divine will intends for me to work," I thought. Since this thought wholly filled my mind, I didn't see the repeated rejections as rejections from another human being. Feeling quite relaxed and unhurried, I just kept on looking for the place where I would be put to work. On returning home, I called on the sick and continued my efforts to familiarize more people with the teachings of Seicho-No-Ie.

Meanwhile, September came, and with it the morning of the fifth day—the day I had promised to leave home. My mother didn't say a word, but I was understandably tense that day. This was because I had begun to feel that the thing I had promised to do was somehow an agreement I had made with God.

"Everything will be decided today," I seemed to hear a voice saying somewhere in my heart. "Where shall I go, then?" I thought as I sat silently, my hands joined in prayer, as was my custom every day. I had been sitting in this position for an hour or so when the word 'Shiba'[16] crossed my mind. "Shiba—who can it be?" The name of a friend, M, drifted hazily through my mind.

"Mother, today is the day we agreed on, isn't it?" I said to her, smiling, as I prepared to go out. My mother was silently gazing at my face. She had been watching me leave every morning and she must have been puzzled to see my cheerful, carefree expression as I announced each rejection, day after day. That morning, as she appeared to be on the point of calling off our agreement, I brought up the subject myself. Seeming unsure of how to react, she only remained silent.

Following the inspiration I had received while praying, I headed toward the K Building, where my friend M worked. Getting off the train at Hamamatsuchō, I headed straight toward the Zojoji Temple. As I turned right after passing through the vermillion-lacquered temple gate, there stood the K Building which I was about to visit.

As I strode along slowly and confidently, gazing up at the sky as usual, it suddenly seemed as though the vermillion-lacquered gate had emerged from within the blue sky. I was continually depicting heavenly images in my mind, and I imagined this vision to be a glimpse of Ryūgūjō, a castle at the bottom of the sea which appears in a Japanese fairy tale. To me, the Zojoji Temple gate truly seemed to tower like an underwater castle. Little did I know that from this month on, for nearly two and a half years, I would pass through this gate every day on my way to work.

When I called on Mr. M on the third floor of the K Building, he welcomed me with a smile. However, since we were fellow poets, all we did was talk about poetry and literature. I didn't even manage to mention that I was hunting for a job. "I'll see you again, and please stop by to visit me at my house, too," I said, as I bid him goodbye.

Forcing a smile as I descended the steps, I thought, "Let's see. I wonder what comes next in the divine plan. What could this morning's inspiration have meant, if not this place? It looks as if I will have to leave home now, but that's all right. Whatever is meant to be will come to pass."

On reaching the ground floor, I stepped outside, but I didn't know which way to walk. I stood at the entrance for a while and reluctantly thought of heading toward the railroad station. I had just taken a few steps in that direction when, suddenly, I heard someone call out:

"Mr. Goi, it's been a long time!" A man of about my own height peered into my face while addressing me with those words.

"Oh, Mr. T! Yes, it's been quite a while. It's nice to see you looking as well as ever," I replied, completely forgetting about my job search for the moment.

While I worked at Hitachi, Mr. T had been editor-in-chief of a monthly magazine for workers, and I had contributed essays and fiction almost every month. He was a close acquaintance.

"Where are you working now?" I asked.

To my surprise he answered, "Right over there," pointing to the K Building from which I had just come.

"Let's go to my office and talk," he said.

With Mr. T leading the way, we turned and headed back toward the K Building. Strangely enough, Mr. T's office was on the third floor, the same floor as Mr. M's. It was located just beyond Mr. M's office, to the right.

"Where were you going today?" Mr. T asked, as he sat down.

"I came to visit Mr. M, who works in the office around the corner from yours. I never expected to run into you." Bit by bit, I was gripped with a sense of excitement. "Undoubtedly I am meant to work with Mr. T," I thought.

According to Mr. T, this building had traditionally been a center for research on economic problems and labor affairs. Now, soon to change its name to the C Building, it was being prepared as the site of a new research project on labor problems and worker education. As assistant to the editor-in-chief, Mr. T worked with the Publications Department and was responsible for publishing a number of monthly magazines.

"If by any chance you're available, I'd like your help," he told me. The conversation then developed as I had felt it might.

I had no objections, of course. "Finally, I can ease my mother's worries," I thought, breathing a justifiable sigh of relief. However, I was not to be hired so easily. The reason for this lay in the religious comments I continually made, regardless of whom I was speaking with.

I gave my resume to Mr. T, and then the head of the Publications Department took me to be interviewed by the vice president, Mr. I. My interview with Mr. I was completed without any problems, and he took my resume to the company's president.

"Mr. Goi, could you start working today?" Mr. T asked, as if I had already been hired. Judging me suitable for the work, he didn't expect to encounter any resistance from his superiors.

During most of our conversation, as soon as Mr. T had finished what he wanted to say, I would instantly direct the conversation to Seicho-No-Ie. I talked about spiritual ray healings, the spiritual world, and the theories of Seicho-No-Ie, which stated that sickness and suffering do not truly exist.

"Is that so? Really? That is interesting." Mr. T would say, listening quietly and nodding. But when it came to the non-existence of sickness and suffering, he showed some resistance to the idea.

"In theory, such a concept may exist, but I can't bring myself to think of it as reality—it is impossible," he objected.

In reply, I reiterated the theory and, naturally, my tone became rather emphatic.

"Well, I don't know. I'm not sure about such things," he answered.

I continued to explain that there really is no sickness, that the physical body does not exist, and that all those things are merely creations of the mind. No matter how much I repeated the theories of Seicho-No-Ie, Mr. T didn't seem to absorb any of it.

"Mr. Goi, let's postpone this discussion for another day and talk about your work here," he said, changing the subject. Mr. I is taking a long time. I wonder what he is discussing with the president," he said, tilting his head as he looked at me.

Aware of my situation once more, I smiled nonchalantly and reminded myself, "That's right. I'm here to talk about a job." After a while, Mr. I came and said, "Sorry to have kept you waiting. Mr. Goi, would you please go to the president's office for a minute? He would like to interview you."

"All right," I replied as I headed toward the president's office.

"Mr. Goi—that's your name, isn't it?" asked the president, a plump, middle aged man with a cheery smile. "Please be seated," he said casually, indicating a chair. Then he asked me some scattered questions about my previous work and my relationship with Mr. T. I answered in the same piecemeal manner. Coincidentally, the president happened to mention a friend's illness. As if I had been waiting for the chance, I jumped in and said, "Sickness is really nothing." Then I talked fervently about healing with the palms of the hands and the non-existence of the physical body.

"Um-hmm," the president murmured, but after listening for a while, he said:

"Young man, it has already been proven scientifically that the physical body gives off electricity. The spirit, or whatever you call it, has nothing to do with it. This claim that the physical body and sickness do not exist is just an abstract concept. Such theories only confuse people. At any rate, thank you for your trouble. You seem to have a rather delicate constitution, so do take care of yourself. That is all."

"Now what have I done?" I thought as I bowed, thanked him, and returned to Mr. T's office.

"What took you so long? What happened? Don't tell me you talked about spiritual subjects with the president," he said, giving me a dubious look.

"I think I made a serious mistake," I said, looking rather crestfallen. Just then, Mr. T received a call from the president asking him to come to his office. Mr. T hurried upstairs. Returning after a while, he said:

"Mr. Goi, what are we to do? You talked so much about your strange ideas that the president doesn't want to hire you. This firm is involved in education and research into economic and labor problems. Most of the people here are materialists. I should have warned you about that, but... anyway... we have a problem," he said with a worried look, as though he were in a real predicament. I felt remorseful about what I had done to Mr. T, as well as ashamed of myself for losing such a good opportunity.

"However, Mr. Goi, the president did not say your theories were wrong. He just said that you seemed to be physically weak, and that you might not be up to the work. So, as long as we can verify that you are healthy and have plenty of stamina, the rest will depend on my efforts. I think I can get you hired," he said, this time more pleasantly. "I'll get your employment record from Hitachi if that's all right with you." He seemed to be waiting for my consent.

"Of course, that will be fine. My attendance at Hitachi was much better than average," I said, fully confident.

Being familiar with my abilities and my disposition from our days together at Hitachi, one way or another Mr. T seemed bent on making me his right hand man. "You can surely expect to receive good news from me!" he said, as I left the office.

My uninvited remarks on spiritual matters were the reason I was not hired immediately, although I did not clearly realize it at the time. I simply thought, "If I can't work at the K Building, that is also the divine will." My only worry was what to tell my mother when I got home. I had not been rejected outright, so I wasn't willing to leave home just yet. "Whatever will be, will be," I thought, as I opened the front door to the house.

"Is that you, Masahisa?" called my mother. "You received a notice about an employment test from someplace."

"Is that so?" I replied, entering the house and picking up the postcard. It was a message requesting me to report to the G Publishing Company for a test at ten o'clock the next morning.

"So, how did it go today?" my mother asked sympathetically. She appeared a little distressed at the thought that I might be leaving home that day having failed to find employment. It was one thing to leave home for the sake of a job, but for me to leave without being employed would surely cause her anxiety. Out of parental love and concern, she had set a deadline for my departure so as to encourage me to find a job and stabilize my lifestyle. Perhaps she felt that as long as I was trying my hardest to find a job, it would be all right to postpone my departure for another ten or twenty days. This seemed to be what my mother was feeling, as evidenced by her consoling manner.

I told my mother about what had transpired that day, adding, "It seems that I am meant to work there, but I wonder what will happen. Well, we'll know in a few days. In any case, tomorrow I will go the place mentioned in the postcard."

That night, as usual, I visited the homes of a few Seicho-No-Ie members to encourage them in their faith. There was a teaching in Seicho-No-Ie that was the opposite of the maxim "Silence is golden; speaking is silver." According to this teaching, words speak louder than actions, and not the other way around. Words of truth should be conveyed to people at each and every opportunity. It was said that every time one conveys such words of truth, one's own faith is deepened.

By that time, I was already well versed in the teachings of Seicho-No-Ie, and knew many of the explanations in the *Truth of Life* books by heart. I would convey these to people, thinking "What a wonderful teaching!" So engrossed was I in this thought that I paid little attention to the reactions of my listeners. I couldn't comprehend why some of them were unwilling to accept such brilliant, true teachings. Those who failed to understand despite my repeated explanations seemed almost absurd to me.

To me, the whole universe was beautiful. Sickness, poverty, and struggle were all shadows of our confused minds and, in actuality, were non-existent. The mere fact of being alive was reason enough to feel thankful at all times.

I was constantly filled with such gratitude that I always felt happy and in good spirits. Whenever I encountered anyone, no matter who it was, I made them listen to me talk about Seicho-No-Ie. I was convinced that no teaching other than that of Seicho-No-Ie could really uplift and awaken people, and I continued to talk about it at every possible opportunity.

The next day, I called at the G Publishing Company, which had sent me the postcard. I was given an examination on Japanese literature and an essay on democracy. The examination on Japanese literature was quite easy, and I was able to write the essay without taking much time. Looking back on it now, I realize that my comments held a decidedly religious tone. I finished the examination in good spirits and left the company in a cheerful mood. However, I did not feel that I would be hired by this firm. I had come only because I had received the notice. I had taken the test, and that was all. That morning, I sensed that my place of employment had already been settled, and I felt relaxed and assured. "Tomorrow, I will devote the day to my work with Seicho-No-Ie," I thought to myself as I read the society's books during the train ride home.

The following morning, a telegram arrived with good news that delighted my mother. It was an employment notice from Mr. T. Quickly, I got ready to leave the house.

Mr. T welcomed me warmly, appearing absolutely delighted. I was to serve as an unofficial staff member for three months and then, depending on my performance, I might join the regular staff. This was the agreement under which I was hired. Mr. T happily explained to me that, although the president had been reluctant to hire me, the attendance records that Mr. T had obtained had put an end to his objections.

I was to serve as a member of the Publications Department of the C Workers' Educational Institution. My job was to publish the *C Workers' Times*. This publication came out three times a month, and it reported on labor statistics, strikes, conferences, the National Employees Union, the Ministry of Labor, the status of foreign workers, and anything dealing with the activities of the emerging labor movement.

The Central Workers' Committee Assembly was also located in the C Building. The assembly consisted of employers, employees, and third party representatives who met frequently to mediate labor disputes. Occasionally, groups of workers gathered in front of the hall, waving red flags and singing union songs to express support for the labor representatives' position. Since our work had a close relationship with this labor committee, a knowledge of labor problems and economics was an absolute requisite.

Not knowing the first thing about economics, I suddenly found myself studying the works of Hegel, Marx, Marsus, and Robert Owen. Since I had always worked in areas concerned with human relations and cultural activities, this was a drastic change for me.

Soon after I started, I realized that I must have been

put to work here in order to study the sphere of materialists. Even more amazingly, another circumstance unfolded which, although I gave it no thought at the time, became a turning point in setting the course of the second half of my life.

This institution was a private foundation composed of five departments. The Research Department was the main body, and the Departments of Publishing, Business, General Affairs, and Public Relations were smaller offices. (Later, a school and a Communications Department were also created.) At the time I was hired, nearly forty people were working there, and that number continued to grow with time.

One day, Mr. T informed me that the day before I began work, a young woman named M from Kameari—the same neighborhood where I lived—had begun working in the Public Relations Department.

"Oh, really?" I replied, not particularly interested. I had dedicated myself body and soul to my new studies and to the Seicho-No-Ie philosophy, and I was not the least bit interested in knowing about anyone's personal characteristics or where they were from. I would talk about Seicho-No-Ie to anyone who seemed friendly, and give them an explanatory pamphlet. It didn't matter who my listener was. I believed that if more people became interested in Seicho-No-Ie and followed its principles, a wonderful new Japan would gradually be born. I believed that each new person to whom I imparted the truth would help to fulfill this mission. I did my work at the institution conscientiously, but to Seicho-No-Ie, I devoted myself heart and soul.

Soon afterwards, the young women who worked at the institution asked me to conduct a choral group. I accepted willingly, but even then I thought to myself in a calculating way, "This may open up more opportunities for me to spread the teachings of Seicho-No-Ie."

During the lunch hour, we borrowed the auditorium to start chorus practices. Nearly ten young women met for the rehearsals. With the exception of the women named T and M, they were all beginners. After practice, I approached Ms. T and Ms. M and said, "Your voices and rhythm are quite steady. You must have sung quite a bit during your school days.

"Yes, my older sister is a singer," Ms. T answered in a self-assured manner. In talking with her more, I discovered that she was the younger sister of a famous soprano singer.

During my conversation with Ms. T, Ms. M had remained silent, with a slight smile and a quiet, somewhat lonely expression on her face. Recalling Mr. T's words, it suddenly dawned on me that this must be the woman from Kameari. I remembered his saying that her name was M.

"Ms. M, you come from Kameari, don't you?" I asked abruptly.

"Yes, that's right. How did you know?" she answered, giving me a quizzical look.

"I heard it from Mr. T. I am from Kameari, too."

"Are you really?" she nodded, then fell silent. As she was a woman of few words, we lost the thread of the conversation, and I changed the subject.

"Let's practice again tomorrow," I said, returning to my office to get back to work.

Publishing the periodical was not so difficult, but the content was limited to labor problems and dealt mainly with various kinds of strikes. The word 'struggle' appeared frequently in the articles.

With a world of great harmony as my ideal, I devoted my inner thoughts solely to the Seicho-No-Ie movement. But like it or not, here in this workplace to which I had been brought, I was absorbing the atmosphere of the postwar labor movement. Here, I had to directly face the swift currents of materialistic society, and determine to what extent I could flow with them without losing my own bearings.

Names such as Tokuda, Shiga, and Yashiro Ii[17] appeared in every issue of the publication, and occasionally I even encountered these people myself.

What a fiery, fighting spirit people have kindled in

their passion to achieve their goal! Under their direction, huge masses of workers leaped into action, joined by those who hated the capitalist class, and by those were desperately struggling to protect their right to exist. Bound together by their pressing will to eat and to live, they went on struggling. The pages of the *Workers' Times* reflected the joyless intensity of their environment, and, through the climate of the Workers' Committee Assembly, it continuously stabbed into my heart.

In our essential reality, I believed, there are no struggles. There is no poverty. There is no suffering. All these things are reflections of human thought. And so, during my free moments at work, I went around explaining this to my co-workers. But the materialists of the Workers' Assembly paid me no heed. Arguments arose with the occasional few who would lend me an ear.

"When people come crying to you that they have no rice to eat tomorrow, would you simply tell them that if they pray to God, their rice will fall from heaven?" they would argue.

"Yes, certainly the rice will fall, but through the hands of another human being," I would answer confidently, and would start to explain the laws that govern our minds. Meanwhile, the other party would become angrier and would dismiss my words as a romantic's dreams. Although they recognized my good nature, other listeners also failed to agree with my assertions.

There emerged a dispute with management over an increase in wages. When I expressed my unwillingness to support a strike, I was told, "Do not talk to us about God. No matter how much we pray, management will not raise our wages. Only through real revolt will our aims be met." People either considered me a fool or attacked me verbally. Even those who did not wish to strike seemed unconvinced by my theories, finding them unrealistic.

Amidst these internal and external conditions, I relentlessly continued speaking to small groups of fellow workers, but the number of my supporters did not grow. The only fruits of my efforts were the four or five women in the choral group who began to subscribe to the Seicho-No-Ie monthly magazine, out of a sense of indebtedness to me.

During this period, I happened to be traveling to work every morning with Ms. M from the chorus. We could not help riding together, since we left from the same station and reported to work at the same time and place. At first, facing each other on the crowded train, we would talk about music and culture, but imperceptibly, I would turn the conversation to the teachings of Seicho-No-Ie.

This young woman had been trained in English at a missionary school in Hiroshima, and her job in the Public Relations Department entailed translating and interpreting. Since she had graduated from a missionary school, she was well versed in stories from the Bible. She herself, however, was not a Christian.

I mentioned that the true nature of a human being is that of a perfect divine child, but that we become confused and express hurtful thoughts, which give rise to suffering. The quiet young woman suddenly objected:

"I find that strange," she said. "If we are perfect beings, why have we projected hurtful thoughts and become confused? It is impossible for any perfect being to be confused."

Other people had occasionally asked me the same question, and I had not yet been able to give a clear answer:

"Because we are whole and perfect, confusion does not exist. But if we believe confusion exists, we become confused in our attempts to clarify it. Our confusion deepens, and our thinking becomes bewildered. Gradually, we withdraw from our divine consciousness and settle into a world created by our own confusion." I would give this kind of dubious reply, which made it seem as if I understood when really I didn't.

"I guess I just don't understand," said Ms. M.

"In other words, it means that this world that we perceive through our five senses does not actually exist. The only thing that exists is the luminous and resplendent world of God. So, let go of your perceptions of this world and let your mind focus on the true universe, the realm of divine consciousness. Only then will you understand the truth of your existence."

"Really? But even so, I still don't understand. The daily sufferings of the people of this world are too great. Doesn't that mean that we are defeated by these sufferings? How can people even successfully imagine the true, complete image of themselves?" Her face grew sad and somber.

"This is not good," I thought to myself. My intention had been to direct the conversation toward a joyful topic to cheer up this quiet, fragile young woman. Instead, it seemed to have provoked the opposite reaction.

"I don't understand why God created such an imperfect human world," she said. "If God is love, why does God let us suffer so? Why didn't God create harmonious beings who can do only good, and who don't create unhappiness?"

I was silenced and speechless. Here on this crowded train were passengers commuting to work every day to support themselves and their households. Some of them, perhaps, were also caring for the sick and the aged. To people like these, theories about perfect and complete beings hold no value. Earning a stable income is their immediate concern. Thoughts of the labor disputes proclaimed in the *Workers' Times* and visions of the masses waving their red flags flickered through my mind.

Both of us remained silent as we walked to the C Building. Even if everyone around me was opposed to my ideas, I didn't think the path I had chosen was wrong. Besides, it didn't matter what Ms. M said. I believed that she was wrong and that my thoughts were correct. However, something inside me was gradually changing. I began to think that one must have some special kind of ability or method to make the theories of Seicho-No-Ie comprehensible to everyone.

Morning after morning, my conversations with Ms. M continued. Actually, I was the one who talked. I repeated the theories of Seicho-No-Ie over and over again. Eventually, Ms. M stopped raising objections to my ideas. This wasn't because she agreed with me, but rather because she realized that nothing she said would make me change my way of thinking. I clearly understood this, but I kept on talking in the hope that my ideas might sink in subconsciously. I was driven by my desire to make her understand the truth of the universe.

For me, only Seicho-No-Ie existed. Imparting the theories of Seicho-No-Ie to everyone was my divinely appointed mission, I thought, and everything else paled in comparison. Of course, I devoted myself to my daily employment, and strove to do a respectable job of editing the news bulletin. However, there was not a great deal I could do, since the contents were already laid out for me. So, I just did my best to see that the publication deadlines were met.

Soon afterwards, the workers' union asked me to conduct the singing of the workers' songs on May Day. These were songs of the red flag and the revolution, and there were also a couple of stirring new workers' ballads. This situation distressed me. Seicho-No-Ie placed great importance on the power of words. Taniguchi Sensei had said, "Japan lost the war because they sang songs such as 'Umi Yukaba,' about death wishes." It was a great blow to me to know that I would have to teach songs of the revolution and the red flag, but I knew it could not be helped. Whether I taught the songs or not, everyone would sing them. So, I decided to teach the songs with the intention of purifying them at the same time.

Finally, on May Day, I was made to stand at the front of the procession heading toward the rally ground, the plaza in front of the imperial palace. My role was to lead the chorus in singing revolutionary songs as we walked. The masses of workers, interspersed with revolutionary agitators, then advanced toward the plaza to the strains of the revolutionary song, red flags waving and ready to break into a violent uproar.

Not knowing the essential nature of human beings, people who find meaning only in the pursuit of material things are like charcoal or firewood. Depending on how fire is used, it can be indispensable to one's home and country. But if a flame is ignited carelessly, it can burn down one's home, and can destroy one's country and all of humanity. If they knew the truth of the human existence, people would not let themselves get close to a fool who is about to set a fire. Instead, they would influence the fool to change his or her mind about doing so. I am still longing for that day, but it is not enough just to wait and hope. We must work to create such a day, as soon as possible.

During the march, I became intensely aware of the fearsome power wielded by masses of people. I also realized that, to be truly effective, a teaching must be able to motivate people to action. At the same time, it must uplift people's spirits and way of life. I began to wonder how many people would join me if I continued to expound on the theories of Seicho-No-Ie.

For the first time, doubts about Seicho-No-Ie crossed my mind. Immediately, I banished such doubts with the thought, "God will re-educate the people through Mr. Taniguchi in a wonderful way that we can hardly begin to imagine."

On that day, I composed this poem:

Amidst the endless march of the people
With the chorus singing songs of revolution

The angel within me cries:
"Who is this who is trying again to lower the value of
     human beings?
In place of bombs and cannons,
Who is this who is robbing the people of their souls?"

Placing heaven below earth,
They aim to suppress light with darkness
Without realizing the injustice of it all.
In this march that diminishes life,
How foolish it is
To waste precious time.

In strife there is no justice,
In hatred there is no peace.
Is even this simple logic
Too difficult to understand?

In the light of the azure sky,
I walk at the front of the chorus.
Amidst the whirlwind of revolutionary song,
I walk along singing:
Oh, dear God... Oh, heavenly angels...
Riding on the melody of a revolutionary song,
I walk along, singing my hymn to the angels.

Starting from that night, there was a slight change in
my daily prayer:

"Dear God, grant me great strength. Let the light of
divine wisdom illuminate the hearts of the people!"

Shedding the Old Self

I am a harmonist. I believe in the power of bright thoughts and I dislike conflict. However, despite my distaste for confrontation, I was once in close contact with words like 'struggle' and 'strife,' reporting daily on labor disputes and strikes. I covered the conditions of workers in various prefectures, writing stories, for example, on how the labor union in a given city had overpowered the management of a facility and taken control of the premises, or how prolonged labor disputes had forced the closure of a given mine. Day after day, I was shown a very dark side of society, and a way of life in which people barely survived.

Life under these conditions was too close to the wire for people to have time to think about spiritual matters. Their only concern was having enough to eat. During the war, it was accepted that everyone's purpose in life was to serve the nation. But now, each individual thought only of his or her own survival. In fact, the general public could no longer afford to think of anything but their own lot. Their sole aim was to improve their material living conditions.

The notion of persevering for the sake of the nation seemed to vanish with Japan's defeat. Even if some sensible people suggested biting the bullet during national reconstruction, those opinions were quickly kicked aside by the urgings of leftist groups to fight for the improvement of the lot of the workers.

Under these circumstances, in a nation without an aim, people could not expect any help from the government. They had no alternative but to look after their own welfare. Apart from a few clear-sighted people, no one had any idea of how they could contribute to their country. The only thing that was clear to everyone was that they could not depend on anyone but themselves. The true sentiment of the general population was that they would welcome anything or anybody—even the Communist Party or foreign control—that would help them get enough to eat every day.

Despite living in this kind of environment, I would go to the Seicho-No-Ie center whenever I had a day off, and after returning home, I would visit people in the neighborhood to talk about the society's teachings. My own thoughts were growing brighter and brighter, but people's hearts were not being illuminated, as I had ardently hoped they would. My explanations of 'light-thought' were fairly effective for the sick, but they hardly proved convincing to those who merely desired a bit more to eat or an escape from poverty.

"Poverty is non-existent. Poverty is a projection of your own mind. God did not give humans poverty. So, your lot will definitely improve if you continue to believe that the phenomenon of suffering is mere illusion." This is how I would explain the Seicho-No-Ie theory that true reality is perfectly harmonious. Among the reactions I received was this fairly reasonable one:

"Is that so? You must certainly be happy if you can think that way. But it's hard for us lay people to accept that idea. Life is much too hard for that."

Most people did not even bother to reply, but merely disclosed a wry smile as they allowed my words to go in one ear and out the other Others would even shout at me:

"You can say these marvelous things because you are single. I have a family to feed, and I certainly don't have time to sit around and digest your sermons."

Thus, all my efforts to spread the teachings of Seicho-No-Ie proved ineffective.

Human hearts are mysterious indeed. Once people enter the framework of an idea, they become completely blind to things outside of it. They start feeling strange about that which others take for granted, or will accept as a matter of course things which seem quite odd to others. The most bizarre examples are to be found in the words and deeds of political extremists and religious enthusiasts, and I was most certainly among the latter.

I was totally convinced of the supreme worth of the Seicho-No-Ie teachings. I was certain that this was the only philosophy that could uplift humanity. My overenthusiasm kept me from observing the shortcomings of the group's ideas, which could be perceived in the words and behavior of many of its members. The teachings themselves were slow to effect any real changes, and if explained erroneously, they could result in arrogance or in hurt feelings.

Proponents of almost any spiritual method have a tendency to exaggerate their tales of the method's successes, and to keep quiet about any failures or troubles which may have arisen due to misunderstandings or incorrect application of the teachings. I, too, had been one of those people. So great was my passion to spread the Seicho-No-Ie teachings and so inflexible was my belief that humanity could be enlightened by this faith alone.

But, seeing the poor results of my efforts, I began to

have doubts. Positive reactions were scarce, and at first I thought my own explanations must have been defective. So, rather than rely on my inadequate manner of communicating the teachings, I decided to pass a copy of the Seicho-No-Ie magazine to everyone I met. About one percent of those to whom I gave copies began to subscribe. Even half a percent would have been enough to make me rejoice, so I was very happy about these people taking up the magazine on their own. This gave me even more satisfaction than visiting and healing the sick.

However, after three to six months, old subscribers began to drop off, and were replaced by new ones. Even the regular subscribers fell into one of two groups: those who continued to receive the magazine simply out of habit, and those who understood the theories it published but could not put their knowledge into practice. The same tendencies could be found among Seicho-No-Ie members in general.

Additionally, there were many who would talk and talk, simply out of a desire to exhibit the elaborate theories they had mastered. Many middle-aged and older people who were otherwise free from any sort of intellectual pretensions would suddenly begin expounding to their friends on the 'law of mind' and the 'non-existence of the physical body,' as if they had developed these theories themselves. Some young people would immodestly show off their knowledge of Seicho-No-Ie theories, even to their seniors who and to learned people.

There were also an increasing number of housewives and mothers-in-law who would feign meekness, saying, "Everything is a projection of my mind. I am to blame for everything," while simultaneously blaming their husbands or their own mothers-in-law, based on the psychoanalytic theory of the 'law of mind.' Though I admired Seicho-No-Ie's ideas, I gradually became less and less able to ignore these tendencies.

On the one hand, Seicho-No-Ie taught that humans are essentially perfect, integral beings, children of God who are free from any trace of sin or corruption. On the other hand, it also taught a type of psychoanalysis described as the 'law of mind,' which was used to point out people's weak points. It was the latter that eventually began to trouble me.

Psychoanalysis, which involves seeking out past injuries in the human heart, is not for people who seek spiritual sustenance; it is better left to scientific specialists called doctors. I feel that for the leaders of Seicho-No-Ie to report psychoanalytic theories in books that everyone can buy, and to explain them in speeches, is particularly dangerous, because those ideas are made available to the public along with the wonderful lectures and books which explain that we have within us a perfectly harmonious true reality, a quality equal to that of God. I say this because people accept psychoanalytic methods into their subconscious without any doubts, as if they were drinking pure water, out of respect for their teacher, thinking, "he makes such splendid, wonderful speeches, so this must be true also."

People were told, for example, that an eye represented a woman, and that eye disorders indicated that a man was doing something wrong in relation to women. A wife who had heard this would worry whenever her husband's eyes bothered him, imagining that he was having affairs with other women. If she had not learned this psychoanalytic theory, she would never have entertained such a notion. There were many situations like this. People may be able to heal illness or make a positive change in their lives once or twice using this approach, but in the long run, a psychoanalytic application of the 'law of mind' fosters a constantly critical attitude towards oneself and others.

"That woman has a bandage on her left leg. She has probably been neglectful of her husband, or has not paid due respect to the people around her."

"My son's wife is always in pain from her hemorrhoids. Maybe she doesn't like living in this house."

This habit of connecting all occurrences of physical pain with faults or dissatisfactions is not just ridiculous— it is a harmful attitude that can easily plunge people into

a mental hell. This pseudo-psychoanalytical way of thinking makes it hard for a person to deal with things which
could normally be handled quite easily. Most importantly,
it greatly obscures one's natural ability to love and forgive.

In my judgment, it is a serious mistake for a spiritual leader to propagate such teachings. Truckling to the
whims of science is the last thing the spiritually-minded
should do. Scientists have a role of boring into the phenomenal world in their search for essential truth, whereas
people of spiritual faith directly grasp the essential truth
and explain it in terms of this phenomenal world. The
two disciplines start from opposite ends and are reunited
later. If people of faith unwittingly shift directions in mid-
stream by hopping onto the bandwagon of contemporary
scientific thinking before the right moment has arrived,
they run the risk of neglecting their original role of intuitively grasping the essential, divine truth.

My own present way of explaining things is that illness and poverty are all the vanishing phenomena of
one's karma from a past consciousness. You need not torment yourself by brooding over mistakes in your past attitude which may or may not have caused your present suffering. Just believe that all your difficulties are occurring
in the process of fading away, and that they will vanish
without fail. After they have vanished, your own innate

divine light will appear, creating truly positive circumstances for you. Firmly assure yourself that everything that appears will eventually disappear, and be thankful to your guardian divinities and spirits, for they will surely arrange everything in the best possible way. This is a method of complete entrustment to the divine, a teaching of unconditional love and forgiveness that does not recognize even one speck of evil in the true nature of a human being.

If we are going to teach that human nature is essentially good, we should teach it from start to finish. Should a spiritual proponent teach something that can be used to dig up human evils and faults, in the manner of modern psychoanalysis, then a spiritual faith that once uplifted people to heaven will suddenly thrust them into hell. For this reason, it is important to avoid superfluous chatter.

It was much later that I formed these kinds of clear criticisms on the approach of Seicho-No-Ie. My respect for Taniguchi Sensei never waned, and whenever I felt troubled by such concerns, I made a conscious effort to reject those feelings. I was convinced that even those who could not comprehend my words or the magazine would certainly be enlightened if only they could meet Taniguchi Sensei. I began to bring people into the Seicho-No-Ie center almost by force.

Ms. M was one of these people. For some reason, I was

more enthusiastic about introducing the teachings to her than to anyone else. I wanted somehow to awaken her to the truth. The unlikelihood of our meeting, one from Hiroshima and the other from Tokyo, and then working together from morning to night, was more than coincidence. Thinking along the lines of Seicho-No-Ie, I believed we must have been deeply connected in some way. The loneliness and melancholy that this young woman carried inside her cast a dark shadow that seemed to negate the joy of life. Her tender and fragile heart seemed to be taking on the entire country's post-war suffering as if it were her own. Her inquiry, "If God is omnipotent, why does God let human beings suffer so?" was the very manifestation of her desire to rescue the human world from its present troubles, and it was also a lament over her own helplessness.

I was confident that her suffering would be relieved by coming in touch with Seicho-No-Ie, and I was certain that it was my mission to rescue her. I recalled these words of Jesus: *If your thoughts twine closely round you, send them to a far distant place.*[18]

One Sunday, after the ginkgo trees had turned bright yellow, I took a reluctant Ms. M to the Seicho-No-Ie center in the Akasaka district of Tokyo, enticing her with the promise of a movie afterwards.

To me, Taniguchi Sensei was a dear and irreplaceable teacher, but to Ms. M he was but one of the world's spiritual leaders. When Taniguchi Sensei's lecture began, her impressions quickly became my only concern. I could listen to his words with reassurance only when she smiled or seemed to be paying serious attention. We filed out among the audience that had packed the hall, and rubbed our feet, which had fallen asleep from a thirty-minute meditation seated on our knees.

On the way to the Aoyama Ichome subway station, I asked her what she thought. She replied, "The speech was very good and well delivered, and I'm sure he is a very learned person, but I did not receive such a strong impression from what he said. Maybe it's because I have been hearing your explanations almost every day, and I've already read all the books you lent me. I have taken in everything you've gone to so much trouble to tell me. But I have my doubts whether human society can actually be uplifted with those kinds of explanations alone. I am sure there are some individuals whose lives will be deeply affected by them, but I wonder if most people have enough leeway in their minds to pay close attention to those kinds of theories."

As she was saying this, I began to feel very angry. She seemed terribly impertinent. "Why can't she be more open to such a brilliant speech? It would do her so much good if she would open up and listen, and then practice what she has learned. Then she would awaken and be an inspiration to the people around her. All she would need to do is to talk with others about her own experiences. But she won't even give this teaching a chance. Such a wonderful teaching..." As I thought about this, my anger changed to sorrow. I walked in silence, with an indescribably unpleasant feeling.

Noticing my unhappy mood, she looked at me and said, "I'm sorry, have I made you angry? I didn't mean to say that Seicho-No-Ie's teachings are bad. I just think it puts itself too high up to solve the difficulties of our daily lives. Please forgive me for saying that. I really appreciate the kindness you have shown in taking me there."

I did not feel like answering her. I thought to myself, "Why am I so concerned about her? Others often express their opposition more strongly, but it never upsets me or gets me down." Suddenly, in my mind I experienced an intense feeling of embarrassment, because the thought came to me that I was in love with her. Then, I quickly banished the thought. Straightening my shoulders, I said to myself, "That's ridiculous. I cannot spare the energy for falling in love! Haven't I already dedicated myself to working for humanity?"

"Why don't we take a walk to Meiji Shrine?" she said, thinking I was still angry.

Recovering a bit of my inner brightness, I said with a smile, "That sounds fine. I wanted to take you to see a movie, but I hardly feel like it now, after receiving your low marks."

A short while later, the two of us were walking in the park outside Meiji Shrine. On both sides of the avenue, the golden leaves of the ginkgo trees waved in the blue sky, while families and couples strolled underneath. The park was filled with natural beauty and peaceful human lives, but my heart was heavy with a sadness that would not go away. Where had it come from? Were the social upheavals of the times bothering me? Yes, to some extent. But it seemed there was some other kind of emotion, suddenly born, that was affecting me even more.

As we sat on the lawn, the two of us looked up silently at the sky. "My heart is not in that sky now," I thought to myself. I saw some cockscombs blooming pure red across the lawn. All at once, a poem came to me:

Over thirty,
In love at last,
It does not burn so violently
As cockscombs in pure red.

Then, I was suddenly overcome by embarrassment at the thought that God had seen me create such a frivolous poem, and my whole body stiffened. I felt emotionally depleted by the shameful feeling that welled up from the bottom of my heart. I had already had one unsuccessful experience relating to the subject of marriage, and was determined not to get married or be involved in a romance, for the sake of my spiritual activities. I had thus disciplined myself to associate with women only at the level of platonic, humanitarian love. Now, I realized that my determination had been miserably broken. I was suddenly no longer the intrepid missionary I had been the day before.

I shut my eyes and prayed to heaven for a while in order to calm myself. "God, please let my mind be one with yours. Please lift this trouble from my heart."

I prayed earnestly many times, as if to wipe off a smudge from my face. It was not until I was speechless, and almost breathless, that a light flashed before my closed eyes and gradually spread down into my heart. I felt shining words that said, "It's all right. All is well. This woman is your wife." It was not like a human voice. It was just something I felt.

Like the heavenly voice I had heard on the banks of the Naka River, the words held an unmovable dignity. Concurrently, the mist which had covered my heart suddenly cleared. My heart grew light, and my innate brightness rapidly returned to me. I opened my eyes and saw Ms. M. She was looking up intently at the sky.

"You really are a quiet person," I said, half amazed at her persistent silence.

"I love being here in nature like this more than anything else. I envy poets. Reading a good poem makes me feel the presence of God. I myself am nothing. I can't do anything," she said with a sigh. She changed the topic to literature and music.

With this change of subject, she became lively, as if a different person. Since her major was English literature, her reading, unlike mine, was not limited to what had been translated. Therefore, when it came to foreign literature, I was obliged to listen. As we talked, thoughts of God and Seicho-No-Ie receded into the background, and the lyricism I once had began to show itself again.

Originally, I am a romantic at heart. It was my admiration for beauty that first led me to study music and literature. This search for beauty naturally turned into a quest for truth and the source of human life. I then plunged myself wholly into spiritual teachings and the awakening of humanity. My whole life was now spent in spiritual pursuits, going to the Seicho-No-Ie center in the morning and practicing meditation at night.

"When you talk about art, I always feel so close to you. You are so warmhearted, so mellow, so filled with love. But when you talk about Seicho-No-Ie, you are like a different person—pushy and stubborn. To be honest with you, I almost feel like running away at those times. I'm sorry if I sound critical, but I really feel that way. I think you have gotten so wrapped up in Seicho-No-Ie that you have pushed your most wonderful qualities deep down into your heart. Everyone in the office feels the same. They say, 'Mr. Goi is so much nicer when he acts like himself.'" Suddenly, she had expressed exactly what she thought of me.

I was astounded by the firm human insight that existed within this woman who, at first glance, appeared meek, soft, and taciturn. She was, and still is, the only person who has ever spoken so truthfully to my face.

Recalling the shining, voiceless vibrations I had received, I determined that they were truly a divine message. Once again, I realized that I needed someone who would give me an opinion from the outside. I needed a critic called a wife.

Communicating with Spiritual and Subconscious Worlds

Thanks to Ms. M's advice and the divine sign I had received concerning our future together, I began to change little by little. I slowly began to see the necessity of retaining my own natural feelings and personality, enhanced by the knowledge I had gained from Seicho-No-Ie, rather than simply conveying the group's philosophy to people and expecting them to swallow it whole, as I myself had done.

In the meantime, I was appointed a Seicho-No-Ie branch lecturer. As my contact with the headquarters increased, I began to get a sense of the discrepancy that existed between the group's ideals and the realistic situation. This discrepancy placed great constraints on the lecturers, at the headquarters as well as at the branches, who were caught between Seicho-No-Ie's vertical principle of perfect reality and its horizontal teaching of the 'law of mind.'

According to the principle of perfect reality, the true nature of human beings is flawless and in perfect harmony. Therefore, at Seicho-No-Ie, we were taught that we must revere all people without acknowledging any negative or discordant elements. Practically speaking, however, this is nearly impossible to do. People who earnestly strove to live by this principle experienced considerable strain, because at all times they had to forcibly persuade themselves that the difficulties which they witnessed daily in human interaction were actually signs of perfect harmony. Yet no matter how hard they tried, they were unable to believe it. Not wishing to reveal this inability to their colleagues, they ended up continually suppressing it and pretending that they could, indeed, see only perfection in the people around them.

In putting up this kind of pretense day in and day out, they gradually fell into a fixed mental and behavioral routine which they applied to all situations. However, since they had not yet become able to perfectly revere all people, or to see all happenings in a positive light, their true feelings were bound to emerge now and then to torment them. As a result, they unknowingly turned into hypocritical people who could not simply be themselves.

The wonderful words given to us upon entering Se-

119

icho-No-Ie, that "the true human existence is perfectly harmonious and there is no such thing as evil," might awaken a few exceptional people to their inner truth. However, in many cases those same words can make people become hypocritical by causing them to pretend to be greater than they presently are.

More and more, I found myself reflecting on this problem. Finally, I formed the opinion that negative conditions exist for everyone except those few who have an unshakable faith in their nonexistence. In view of this, I came to feel that it might be more effective for people to regard all evil and disharmony as the vanishing traces of human beings' karma, appearing in order to fade away and vanish. Although this explanation might not bring about sudden enlightenment, it would not torment people who sought the truth or transform them into hypocrites. Step by step, thoughts like these were taking shape in my mind.

Seicho-No-Ie was trying to help people eliminate their real-life difficulties by having them identify the errors (evils) in their past ways of thinking. This was the horizontal theory of the 'law of mind.' At the same time, it informed people of their essential truth through the vertical principle of perfect reality. I felt that this dual approach led all but the most brilliant or enlightened to confuse the world of truth with the world of material phenomena.

From the very start, I applied the principle of perfect

reality alone, without paying much attention to the 'law of mind.' Once in a great while, I did find myself reflecting briefly on this 'law of mind,' in wondering what sort of past attitude might have been at the source of a particular problem or illness. However, I never ascribed much importance to such thoughts. By and large, though, this 'law of mind' was being used in a way that intensified the pain in people's hearts.

Seicho-No-Ie's teachings described human beings in two ways: the true human being and the human being of phenomenal reality. It was said that the former is the only true existence, while the latter is actually nonexistent. However, people unconsciously tended to give their attention to teachings concerning the superficial, phenomenal side of human life because it was easy to understand and appealed to their curiosity. On the other hand, the reality of human nature, or the idea of human beings as totally united with God, was not so easy to grasp. And so, people ended up finding fault with others, and with themselves, saying such things as, "The reason why this problem has emerged in the physical world (the world of cause and effect) is that you have been harboring a certain attitude." With all this blaming and judging going on, the image of the true human being, which is perfect and harmonious, was forgotten by the wayside, and it was no longer even clear whether human nature was fundamentally good or bad.

Did Seicho-No-Ie's teachings mistakenly assume that the general population had already evolved to the level of near-saints, who could instantly direct their minds only toward the good? In those days, my doubts on this point were not clearly formed.

In mid-January of 1948, I was informed by Ms. Koda of a psychic meeting of the C Society that was to be held at a Mr. Y's house, and I became a member of it. The C Society had branched out from the Society of Psychic Science. It had recently been started by a medium named H and a Dr. S.

I had been attending experimental meetings held by the Society of Psychic Science, in which we witnessed a megaphone flying in the air, a desk quaking, and occasionally, even the audible voices of spirits. Yet, no matter how many times you observe such phenomena, you only gain a recognition that the spiritual and subconscious realms exist, and that human life continues in these realms. Witnessing these phenomena does not bring you in touch with the reality of God. I wanted more than ever to visit a place where higher divinities and spirits might emerge.

In Seicho-No-Ie itself, there was no use of prophetic or precognitive powers. People's questions were addressed with a mixture of theory and personal experience. However, its proponents were not able to provide clear-cut advice that would resolve people's realistic problems. Because their only guidance method consisted of offering general theory in response to each situation, they were obliged to give lengthy lectures. After that, one simply prayed for the other party's problem to be resolved. But unless people receive inspired guidance, they are often left feeling unsatisfied. Therefore, after going to see a Seicho-No-Ie instructor, people often consulted clairvoyants, for better or worse, in search of more clear-cut answers. As a result, having been unable to resolve their problems through Seicho-No-Ie and visits to clairvoyants, quite a number of people fell prey to unscrupulous religious organizations.

When it comes to facing actual problems, most people aren't satisfied with abstruse religious theories, no matter how many times you repeat them. If people need money for tomorrow's living expenses, rather than reciting a religious doctrine, it is often better to confer with them on how they might call on the help of their friends. Every time I was asked for help with this kind of everyday problem, I felt dissatisfaction and even distress over the inadequacy of relying on the Seicho-No-Ie theories alone.

In those days, I was practicing the *shinsokan* prayer every morning and night. I gradually spent more and more time engaged in this prayer, and was becoming more deeply immersed in it. I was beginning to see souls and spirits moving about in front of my closed eyes. Occasionally, my joined hands would shake, or I would receive moments of inspiration, but my spiritual perceptions were still negligible. Since May Day that year, I had been strongly wishing to obtain some kind of superlative ability in order to rescue others from their sufferings. Without my perceiving it, the thought "You are a person who will exhibit power" entered my mind, plunging me into a more concentrated meditation.

Unlike the Society of Psychic Science, the C Society was not intended for scientific studies of spirits. It was a cooperative organization encompassing the divine, spiritual, and human worlds. It had both political and spiritual objectives, and its members were closely linked by their common wish for the rebuilding of Japan and the safeguarding of the world. Among its members were a fair number who were involved with Seicho-No-Ie. It seemed that they had come because they were not entirely satisfied with an approach built on theory alone. For my part, I was still wholly committed to Seicho-No-Ie, but I eagerly desired some other power that would make up for its less-than-adequate approach to people's realistic problems.

Had I been satisfied to seek only my own spiritual awakening, I think that, in those days, I would have already attained that state. I imagine that my awakening was what in Buddhist terms is called a 'passive enlightenment.'[19] This is because I personally harbored no dissatisfactions whatsoever, and was living each day with only the deepest gratitude toward heaven, the earth, and the universe. I was in the perfectly liberated state of having entrusted everything to the divine. I no longer lived for the sake of my individual self. And this mental freedom, or liberation from the self, naturally placed me in the position of an 'active enlightenment,'[20] by taking on all the sufferings of my own country and of humanity as whole. I clearly felt that Japan's troubles were my own, and that humanity's suffering was also my own. My individual ego did not exist. The only place where my consciousness existed was in Japan and the world of human beings.

In those days, my incessant prayer was, "God, please use my life well for Japan and humanity! Please give me a strong power to do this work." This feeling never left my mind.

The psychic meeting of the C Society at Mr. Y's home was held in a Japanese-style room with an area of twenty *tatami* mats (30.61 m^2). Before the meeting, some applicants were given a set of tablets. On these, spirits and divinities were to write messages to each individual. The medium named H held one end of a bamboo pole, while the applicant grasped the other. Then, a bamboo brush, attached to the center, began to move by itself. Words appeared on the tablet beneath the brush. On mine was written: "A hundred pieces of knowledge cannot match a single deed of truth" and "Sincerity and deeds of truth are superior

125

to all knowledge." I clearly recall that these words later proved extremely useful to me.

Once the tablets were distributed, the psychic meeting commenced. To encourage the psychic phenomena to come forth, all joined in singing the Song of Iroha and the Song of Bamboo,[21] followed by the playing of a Japanese song on the phonograph. A clergyman named H conducted the ceremony.

Sitting inside a cabinet made of black cloth, the medium H fell into a trance. The session began just like those of the Society of Psychic Science. A megaphone, a doll, and a desk, all illuminated by phosphorus, flew about in the darkness. Then, a spirit called K spoke to us through the megaphone. The spirit explained that it was a friend of the medium H and was the soul of a young man who had died before his time. After this, the spirit of a hermit named O, who was said to have lived over a millennium and a half ago, gave a talk on how to live on one's true spiritual path. The hermit had been a trained ascetic who had disappeared from this Earth without leaving a trace, not even his physical remains.

All events were carried out under the direction of the hermit. It was explained that he worked within the divine world under Prince S, a central figure, along with many other inhabitants of divine and spiritual realms. Their goal was to uplift human beings residing in this physical world. The hermit talked not only through the mega-phone, but directly through the air. He had a deep voice and used an archaic dialect that was difficult to under-stand. He spoke through the ectoplasm of the medium H (ectoplasm is a substance that contains material and ethe-real elements), and instantaneously gave brief answers to various questions posed by the clergyman H and Dr. S, who was also present.

That day, I learned only a little about the C Society and the mission of the hermit O, but I felt no doubts about the meeting. I simply believed in the words of the presenter and the spiritual beings, thinking that this might serve as a springboard for the fulfillment of my mission. The chilly January evening air refreshed my heart as I walked home.

That night, when I began the *shinsokan* prayer as usual before going to bed, I realized that I could fall into medita-tion very quickly. I saw souls passing in front of my closed eyes. They did not resemble ghosts, but were floating in front of me like Jack o' Lanterns. They were mainly col-ored blue. As I watched them, my hands absent-mindedly began to move. I let them follow their course. The vibra-tions gradually grew more and more forceful, my hands rising above my head or moving horizontally or diago-nally, as if I were cutting through water.

Suddenly, the idea hit me that I could utilize these sorts of spiritual gestures and movements to communicate with the spiritual world. Looking back on it now, I cannot help thinking how rash and foolish I was, but from that night on I was driven onto a path of indescribably rigorous spiritual training. This path may have been necessary for me to reach my present state. However, when I think back on the agony I suffered in those days, I earnestly wish for those who come after me to be able to take a less demanding path to their awakening, and one that simultaneously enables them to benefit others. This desire has become the basis of my present teachings and methods.

By that time, I believed that I was well-informed about psychic phenomena, having repeatedly seen such things myself and also having met many ascetics and mediums and read books from Seicho-No-Ie as well as translations of foreign books. But this was the first time I had actually experienced such phenomena with my own body. With my hands joined together, my arms waved through the air like a huge snake or dragon lifting its head or splashing through the water with its immense tail.

Today, if I were to see someone conducting such training, I would immediately warn them, "Please stop, or your body will become completely occupied by possessing souls!" However, at that time, I did not feel I was in the least danger, and I began to have an unspoken conversation with the spiritual world. "I would now like to talk with you," I said. Shake my hands up and down if your answer is 'yes;' shake them horizontally if you mean 'no.'" As soon as I had formulated that thought, my joined palms were immediately rocked up and down. Yes. "Then, are you human beings?" I asked. Yes. "Are all of you human?" No. "Are some of you fox spirits?" No. "Are some of you dragon deities?" Yes.

The questions and answers continued in this way until about three o'clock in the morning. As a result, I was told the following, regardless of its actual validity: The blue souls appearing in front of me during meditation were high spirits. Five spiritual beings—guardian spirits—were constantly protecting me from behind, and one of them was a dragon deity. Dragon deities are united with human beings in order to help with the flow of our destiny.

It was also explained that I was to work extensively as a pioneer in large-scale, divinely ordained activities. Detailed truths remained to be known, since the answers given were only to 'yes' or 'no' questions. Moreover, the movements I took to mean 'yes' and 'no' may very well have been caused by my own subconscious. Although there was no assurance as to the truth of the answers, there was undoubtedly someone behind me who belonged to a spiritual realm, because my body had moved automatically, regardless of my intentions.

My psychic meetings continued the following night, and the night after that. Before long, I began feeling inclined to meditate even during my working hours. I occasionally demonstrated psychic movements or made predictions to my colleagues in the publishing department, but all these predictions proved to be incorrect. People in the office were beginning to think that Mr. Goi was finally starting to lose his marbles. I, on the other hand, determined that my ridiculous predictions were a good sign. I thought, "Even low-level human and animal spirits can predict trifling, everyday matters because they live in the subconscious world, which is close to the atmosphere of the physical world. The fact that my predictions proved wrong means that I am surely dealing with high-level spirits. Being of high status, they intentionally led me astray in order to admonish me for engaging in such foolishness."

In addition to having these personal psychic meetings, I went wherever a psychic assembly of the C Society was being held. On one of those days, I thought I might try automatic writing. At every spare moment, I would hold a pencil to paper, and wait for my hand to move. Yet, although the act seemed to be driven spiritually, nothing meaningful came of it. Even when I was made to write some words, it was obvious to me that they were the contents of my subconscious and not a correspondence with the spiritual world.

Then one night, I suddenly felt like writing with a traditional brush, and I held a piece of paper in front of me.

After I had meditated for a while, the brush in my hand began to move, very quietly. My hand dipped the brush into the pool of ink on the inkstone, and wrote the name 'Sadao Watanabe' in a wonderfully angular calligraphy.

Holding the brush in my hand, I exclaimed to my mother and brothers, "Look! It's Watanabe! Sadao has returned to us!" My mother and brother, who stood next to me, looked timidly at my desk. My elder brother came in from the next room. This was a style of penmanship that the whole family remembered very well.

"That certainly is the hand of Watanabe! You're right!" my brothers shouted at once in surprise.

It was truly the name of my long-time friend from childhood, my best friend until the mid-war period. Watanabe had been extremely good at fine arts and using the brush, and years ago had made an impression on the whole family. I took the writing instrument into my hand once again. The same name was drawn out in his semi-cursive style, followed by the names "Toshio Goi" and "Masahisa Goi." Toshio is the name of my elder bother, who was then standing by my side. I had once asked Watanabe to inscribe Toshio's name on a doorplate for him. When we compared this to what I had just written, we found the writing to be exactly the same.

"This is surely the script of Watanabe," my brother stated, deeply moved.

Amazed at having seen automatic writing for the first time, my little brother asked, "Is this a communication from the spiritual world?"

"If so, does this mean that Watanabe is dead?" inquired my older brother.

"I guess so," I answered. I touched my right shoulder with my left hand, overcome with a feeling of nostalgia. Watanabe was there behind me, using my body. The feeling that surrounded me was inexpressible. My right hand began to wiggle, as if urging me to write again. I once more took the brush into my right hand. This time, a picture—a portrait—was drawn.

"It's Goro, it's Goro!" my brothers exclaimed.

"It sure looks like him," said my mother, who was observing from behind.

"Mother, it's me, Goro. I'm glad to see you are well. I'm fine, too, and am happily at work." These words appeared beside the portrait, now in a writing that looked exactly like that of Goro, my younger brother who was reported to have been killed in New Guinea during the war.

I felt a little fatigued, and put down the brush. "Two deceased people are living behind me. They appear to be alive and well, living in a world behind this one. The letters and the picture from the spiritual world appeared to float before my eyes in pure black, making me feel that a previously unseen realm had suddenly been revealed to me.

Departing from the Realistic World

Automatic writing continued for me from that night onward. My ears also became spiritually attuned to the point where I could hear the voices of spiritual or ethereal beings as if they were ordinary human voices.

The main content of my automatic writing could be summarized as follows: The time was drawing near when great divine work would be carried out. This work had been planned through a large-scale cooperative effort among the divine, spiritual, and physical worlds. Joining this work from the spiritual and divine realms were various beings whose names were indicated. Those participating from the physical world were named, and the list also included the contributions of well known individuals from the past.

Actually, I didn't place much importance on what I wrote in these sessions. This was because all the events and names that appeared in my writings could be found within my own thoughts, and having written them down did not have any particular influence on my own actions. I suspected that these communications themselves did not mean much—that they were simply exercises in smooth communication between my physical body and the spiritual realm. Whatever their purpose, I did not experience any misgivings or uneasiness about doing these writings.

Perhaps this was because the first people to appear in these spiritual writings were my closest friend Sadao Watanabe and my younger brother Goro. To me, it looked as if all the writing was Watanabe's, disguised to look like it came from different hands. And so, I decided to entrust everything to the spiritual world, and to let Watanabe and Goro use my physical being as they wished. In my mind, I conveyed this to them.

Whether at home or at the office, I spent every spare moment writing words and drawing pictures with my brush. In the end, it became extremely difficult for me to write in my own handwriting with my own will; I needed to exercise great willpower just for editing and reading books. Ms. M and people in the publishing department were serious in their warnings: "Mr. Goi, what you are doing is dangerous. We want you to stop it. You could end up going insane." Ms. M's concern seemed especially grave. With a sad expression, she would say to me, "Why don't you at least visit Taniguchi Sensei once to consult with him about the pictures and written characters you have made?"

By this time, I had already asked Ms. M to marry me, but our plans were still unformed because of her parents' objections. Therefore, we were spending time with each other just as we had before I proposed to her. Nothing further developed. For my part, however, I was absolutely certain that I wished and needed to marry this woman, and I considered it only a matter of time before the matter would be settled. In any case, the pressing demands of the spiritual phenomena I was experiencing were taking up all my energy, and so I set the matter aside for the time being.

As for Ms. M, she was hoping that I would live like an average person, making a living in the field of culture. It seemed to make her terribly uneasy and depressed to see me getting involved in the area of spirits and souls, which was, to her, a totally unknown world. She would always listen to me talk about such matters with a sad and down-hearted expression.

She never tried to stop me from what I was doing, since she was well aware from all the time we spent together that I was not a person who would change my mind in the face of opposition. Still, she kept hoping that my behavior would return to normal, both in words and actions, so that she could persuade her parents to consent to our marriage. Her parents were concerned that my speech and behavior were too far removed from what was considered normal, and that my future was very uncertain. In a nutshell, they feared that we were likely to end up living in poverty. Seeing my unusual daily behavior, hardly distinguishable from insanity, Ms. M could not help but advise caution.

Ignoring her advice and the advice of others, I would lightly reply by saying, "I am all right, there is no problem." Even so, I could clearly sense that my physical condition made it too hard for me keep working in the office.

During that period, I visited Mr. Y almost every evening, giving him advice based on my spiritual intuition. He was considering becoming independent from Mr. Mokichi Okada and continuing to offer his home for the C Society's meetings. Mr. Y, in turn, would suggest to me that I stop working and devote myself entirely to spiritual training, adding that I could stay at his home if I liked. Also, the ascetic named O from the C Society recommended that I become a clairvoyant by practicing automatic writing as often as possible.

Finally, conditions became such that I felt obliged to

begin full-scale training as a clairvoyant. From that time onward, a number of mysterious events began to occur, one after the other. Here, I will describe a few of them as examples.

One evening, in the town of K, there was to be a debate between some Communist Party members and adherents of Seicho-No-Ie. I had been invited to attend this debate as an observer. Since an additional speaker was needed, the Seicho-No-Ie participants asked for the presence of a speaker who had psychic capabilities. At the debate, a heated discussion developed over the differences between the materialistic realism of communist ideology and the Seicho-No-Ie style of abstract idealism. And of course, since these were completely opposing theories, there was no way either side could be convinced by the other.

In the end, the Communist side proposed a difficult challenge: "God and the spirits about which you talk can be neither seen nor touched. We need no more discussion. Here and now, we want to see a visible demonstration of what you call divine miracles." The Seicho-No-Ie lecturers fell silent for a time and watched my face. They wanted me to produce a miraculous feat that would somehow breach this impasse.

To me, the situation seemed difficult indeed. It was not right to produce a supernatural feat for the group which wanted to test God, and as a person of faith, I did not want to do such an irresponsible thing. However, on its own, my right hand began to rap lightly on my knee, signalling the start of an episode of automatic writing. "Go to the center of the room; we will astonish them," I heard.

I decided to follow the suggestion from the spiritual world. I said to the Communists, "All right, I will give it a try." I went to the center of the room, placed a cushion on the floor, and sat down casually on it. Both the Seicho-No-Ie members and the Communists had their eyes on me to see what kind of feat I was going to perform. It was a Japanese-style room, and the people in front of me gathered together at either end of it to leave space for me. I closed my eyes and meditated for a while, sitting on my folded legs.

I had no idea at all what I was going to do, even after having come to the center of the room. Since everything was up to the spirits, I had no alternative but to wait with my eyes closed for their instruction. After shutting my eyes for one or two minutes, I heard a voice from within my head saying, "We will now begin. Open your eyes and keep smiling, with your hands on your knees." It was at that moment that my body started to levitate above the floor, floating here and there, with my cushion still stuck to my body. The audience gazed at me in astonishment. It was odd enough just to see me levitate in a sitting position, but I rose almost a meter above the floor, still seated on the cushion.

The Communists were too stunned to continue the discussion and reach any concrete conclusion that night. Concerned that they might take such strange behavior as the essence of religion, I said, "What I have just now done has nothing to do with spiritual faith. I simply allowed the souls and spirits working in me to prove that there is power in the unseen world as well as in the visible one. I tell you absolutely that this was not done directly by a divine power. In fact, such things can easily be done, even by unenlightened souls. Often, these delinquent souls surprise others by performing uncanny feats of this nature, so I hope you will not get the wrong impression. I feel embarrassed about having given you such a peculiar demonstration, and I hope you will not develop an interest in such things. What I hope is that you will put all your effort into bringing out your divinity as soon as possible, deepening your belief in yourselves in your daily life." At the time, I never dreamed that the Seicho-No-Ie headquarters would later utilize this incident in constructing a criticism of me.

After that, a friend and I paid a visit to an acquaintance. Unfortunately, that person was not home and the fence gate was locked. We decided to wait for a while, because my friend definitely wanted to see this person before the day was out. We waited by the fence at the side of the house, not wanting to stand right in front of the gate. While we were standing there talking, my automatic writing started up again, conveying the message: "Isn't it a bit boring to just stand here? Let's give a surprise to your friend. It will serve as a good experience for you to realize that people in the spiritual world can do such things. Listen carefully; you will hear the gate open." Immediately, we clearly heard the gate open with a rattle.

"Ah, Mr. H has returned home." Saying this, my friend hurried to the gate, but returned and said, "That's strange. The gate surely opened just now, didn't it, Mr. Goi?"

"You're right. I'm sure I heard that sound, too." My tone remained serious as I struggled to suppress a smile. After hearing the sound several times, my friend began to feel uneasy and suggested that we come back another time. It was at this time that the owner of the house actually returned. Apparently, the sound of the gate opening was an artificial sound coming from the spiritual world.

Another example occurred while I was on business in the Ginza district of Tokyo. I used the occasion to take a walk and found myself near the Allied Forces' General Headquarters. At the entrance to the building stood a U.S. soldier and three Japanese guards. As I walked up to them, an inner spiritual voice spoke to me as clearly as a human voice: "Let's go inside. They will not notice you."

In those days, I was determined to do anything and everything that was suggested to me by the spiritual world, so I passed in front of the guards without any hesitation and entered through the gate. The guards certainly were looking in my direction, but they let me by without saying anything. After walking around inside the gate for a while, I returned to my original place. The spiritual voice said, "This time they will notice you." Sure enough, a surprised guard at the exit exclaimed, "Hey! How did you get in here?"

I could hardly keep myself from breaking into laughter, and said, "I passed right in front of you."

"That's ridiculous! Nobody came this way. Isn't that right?" the confused guard asked his colleague. The other guard also had a puzzled look on his face, saying that he too had seen no one. In the end, they nearly begged me to forget the whole incident, because it was a grave matter for them to have allowed a stranger to enter without even a security check. It might even have caused them to lose their jobs. I easily acceded to their request and left the premises.

On my way back, when I asked the spirits why they had brought about such mischief, they answered, "It was to give you a useful experience. It shows that miraculous things can happen when one is in a tight spot."

While living this way, I suddenly had a disquieting

thought: "What should I do if I discover that these spirits and souls are not ones with a divine mission, after allowing them to deprive me of my free will?" This was followed by another apprehension: "What should I do if what I took to be my friend and my brother turn out to be well-disguised fakes?" Having relinquished my free will, I wouldn't be able to control my own circumstances in the future.

After shuddering over several more of these unsettling thoughts, I looked deep into my own heart and remembered that I had already offered up my life completely to God. I recalled that it was a deep wish to work for the peace of humanity that filled my whole being, and I affirmed to myself, "God would never lead a person who lives with such pure intentions along a wrong path." I then flung away all my worries and resolved to entrust myself body and soul to God. Once I had let go of my worries, my natural optimism quickly returned, and with it the brightness of my heart.

By the end of February, however, I became totally unable to do office work, and resigned from my job, having decided to devote myself to spiritual development at Mr. Y's home. My letter of resignation was written completely by automatic writing. I also gave presents to the young staff in the publishing department as farewell gifts, among which was a very well-drawn picture. It was a slightly profiled portrait of a girl with braided hair. I gave it to a young man named O, saying, "As a parting gift, I would like to offer you this little sketch of the person you love." I later learned that the girl in the picture looked exactly like the girl O was in love with. This was another piece of innocent mischief on the part of my angelic messengers.

The Trials of Spiritual Training

Before forming a new spiritual approach with Mr. Y, I felt that I should first meet with Taniguchi Sensei. I was, after all, a lecturer with Seicho-No-Ie, and was in no way at odds with the organization. I was sincerely engaged in studying the potential of psychic abilities, because it seemed to me that adding this facet to the Seicho-No-Ie method would surely make it a perfect spiritual organization. I felt certain that once my psychic capabilities were fully developed, our group would exert a positive influence on other spiritual groups, and all of them, along with us, would unite with Seicho-No-Ie. It was my intention to put all my effort into working for this goal.

I thought it important that I talk the matter over with Taniguchi Sensei. Without the consent of the spiritual side, though, my body would not move at all. Luckily (or so I thought), my wish was granted and a date was set for me to call on him. Taniguchi Sensei would rarely meet anyone at his home, except for the chief lecturers from his central *dōjō*. However, if I had met with him at the *dōjō*, it would have been impossible to have an in-depth conversation with him there. So, I had no alternative but to visit him at his home. Since, at the conscious level, I had no way of knowing what date would be most propitious for a visit, I decided to leave everything to my spiritual guides and to proceed according to their instructions.

The day designated by the spirits was also the day of a meeting between Taniguchi Sensei and the leaders of the Shirahato Society.[22] The meeting was about to end when I arrived. When I asked to be taken to Taniguchi Sensei, the housekeeper led me to his sitting room without a moment's hesitation. After I had stood waiting for a while, my dear teacher came out from the back room with a puzzled look on his face. "How on earth did the housekeeper let you in here?" he asked without even sitting down. "I said I was not to be disturbed. What is it that brings you here?"

I plunged directly into the subject, earnestly describing my present hopes and way of thinking, and showed him some examples of my automatic writing. I explained that I wanted to fully develop my psychic capabilities, and

145

asked if it would be possible to do so without resigning from my post as a Seicho-No-Ie lecturer.

"I don't see any problem with your doing both at the same time. You can stay on as a lecturer," he replied summarily, as if to urge me on my way. I quickly made my exit, thinking that I should not take up any more of his time.

Standing on the train on my way home, I had begun to meditate when I heard a deep, solemn voice—the Buddhist recitation of a perfectly enlightened being—arising from a place around my heart. "*Namu-Amidabutsu, Namu-Amidabutsu, Namu-Amidabutsu,*"[23] resonated the sound of the serene, dignified voice. It sounded very much like the voice of a well-known high priest who had been deeply respected during his lifetime. I reached home, still listening to the words resonating in my chest. It seemed that I was the only one who clearly heard this voice.

My whole family, save for my younger brother, were skeptical about the existence of souls and spirits, and they appeared worried about my behavior, which was starting to diverge from the beaten track. All my actions were done in accordance with instructions from an unseen world, regardless of whether those instructions had any truth to them or not. To all appearances, I was just like a person possessed by a ghost. "What on earth is this all about?" they wondered. "Without even the slightest sign of regret, he quit a perfectly good job that took a lot of effort to get." To my mother, brother, and sister-in-law, who were leading their daily lives in all earnestness, my every action must have appeared eccentric and even dangerous.

For several days after I quit my job, I commuted to Mr. Y's to help him perform therapy, or to meditate. On my way home, however, I never failed to visit Ms. M at her office or at her home in Suginami (she had moved to that area in the winter of the preceding year). Since the spirits working behind me were again instructing me to marry Ms. M, I was trying to find a way to make her understand my present circumstances and my mission in life.

At all times, my right hand, which was so often occupied in automatic writing, would rap persistently on my knee, describing something or other. It was like a strange habit, or a tic, that would appear while I was walking along the street or talking to someone. Seeing my incessantly moving fingertips and my sudden mood shifts (I would occasionally appear to be listening to a voice from thin air), Ms. M was almost constantly in tears. In seeing this, I recalled the words that appeared in my automatic writing: "This woman is becoming increasingly purified."

Everything I said was concerned with the world beyond, and all the people of whom I spoke were also of other worlds. To Ms. M, a woman seeking truth, goodness, and beauty in this world alone, and who was indifferent to other worlds, most of my words could only seem like signs of insanity. She must have felt immense compassion and an unbearably deep sorrow at seeing her loved one like this, steadily going mad.

Presently, it was decided that I would stay at Mr. Y's house. On the evening before I moved there, I attended a gathering of the C Society with my mother. She had agreed to go, despite the wry smile she gave upon hearing of my spiritual guides' assurance that my deceased brother, Goro, would be there. The meeting was mainly devoted to predictive admonitions about natural disasters by the hermit O, and neither the voice nor any image of Goro made an appearance. My mother was not too disappointed, as she had expected as much, but she was extremely worried about my future. However, her spirits were lifted by the words of Mr. Y, who said, "You are indeed lucky to have such a good son. He is one of the specially chosen people." When, in my heart, I inquired as to why Goro had not made himself known to us, I could feel only the smiling thoughts of the spirits and souls around me.

My life at Mr. Y's home commenced the next day, and a daily routine was soon established. I would first perform a purification for each visitor, and then Mr. Y would complete the process. Prior to the treatment, I would intone the sound 'O—m' in a loud and drawn out voice. This served as a sort of pathway for the descent of divine energy, or a call for perfection. This sound was produced quite naturally and spontaneously. Since I had been a singer, my voice was considered good in terms of projection and resonance. Often, people were healed just by hearing the intonation. Also, since I was exhibiting the power to know and foretell the future, a lot of people had started asking me a variety of questions about problems they faced in their own lives.

Mr. Y, who had welcomed me at first, gradually became wary. He was a warmhearted, expansive person, and he also had courage. Even so, he must surely have felt a strong reluctance to let another person encroach on his territory, established over so many years of effort. Perhaps this was one reason why he felt the need to caution me about the Seicho-No-Ie style of my talks, saying, "Mr. Goi, please stop talking like the people at Seicho-No-Ie. They are not such a good lot."

The voices behind me paid no attention to this, saying, "You only have to endure it for a little while longer. You will soon be leaving him." In any case, it seemed to me that Mr. Y's apprehensions were perfectly natural.

A number of rather strange phenomena occurred during my stay at Mr. Y's home. A hanging scroll in an alcove would flap in the air as I held my palms up before it in prayer. A fine fragrance would permeate the room, as if in blissful celebration of the healing of a certain patient. The face of the little statuette of the *Kannon* goddess[24] would suddenly transform into that of a hermit or a Buddhist monk, and even reflect glorious colors. These events were not only subject to my own perception; they were witnessed by others around me.

One day, I was informed that one person in our group had gone mad and urgently requested that I go to see him. Accompanied by Mr. Y, I arrived at a rural village in Saitama Prefecture at around ten o'clock in the evening. Although I had never been to the place before, I automatically led Mr. Y to our destination, walking along a dark, winding path among the rice paddies.

On another occasion, I found a blue-bronze statue of the *Kannon* goddess among about six images of the Buddha placed in Mr. Y's alcove. I abruptly said to Mr. Y, "This is a carving of the *Kannon* of the Dawn, and it is my own guardian divinity.[25] I wonder, would you mind giving it to me?"

Mr. Y easily fell in with my wish, replying absentmindedly, "Oh, that'll be fine. You can take it."

I immediately left Mr. Y's with the *Kannon* statue, saying, "I must go to my parents' home now to apply for a change of address certificate. I'll see you later." But I never returned there again. On the evening of the day when I returned to my parents' home, I placed the *Kannon* in an alcove in my six-mat (9.18 m²) *tatami* room. The alcove was located at the west side of the room, facing east, and at the north side, facing south, was our family ancestral altar.

Before going to bed, it was customary for my mother to recite a Buddhist invocation (the *Nembutsu*[26]) in front of the altar, while I meditated silently. That night, as usual, my mother burned incense before the altar and started her recitation. After a while, she suddenly stopped and said surprisedly, "It's strange, Masahisa. The smoke of the incense is shining and reaching straight down to the *Kannon* statue." I opened my eyes and looked at the statue. Sure enough, the blue smoke from the high altar came shining in a straight ray about 30 centimeters wide, reaching the *Kannon* figure down in the alcove.

This was a mystery, but I was hardly surprised, having grown accustomed to the mysterious by that time. I was sure that the image in this statue must have been deeply related to me, since I had suddenly requested it even though it was in another person's possession. I recalled that my guiding spirits had referred to it as the image of my guardian divinity, calling it 'the *Kannon* of the Dawn.'

When I searched in my heart for an explanation, I was given the following answer: "This statue was created to

151

symbolize your life's mission as 'the *Kannon* of the Dawn,' and it is strongly linked to your ancestors. That is why you received it from Mr. Y. The meaning of 'dawn' as it is used here is that today's world is dark and wild, and that you will soon manifest the work of the *Kanzeon* Bodhisattva,[27] who invites the dawn and brings light to the world of night. The reason for the shining fumes of incense emanating toward the *Kannon* image is that the joyfulness of your ancestors was reflected in the smoke."

This may sound very odd to those who have not experienced any psychic phenomena, but actually, this kind of occurrence is fairly common. That was all for that night, and I soon fell asleep. But the very next day, I was to embark on my most rigorous ordeal yet, one that would pin me at the verge of sanity and insanity, and of life and death, for the next few months.

Despite the fact that my body was no longer under my own control, I still could not get a clear perception of the spiritual group that was utilizing it. The heavenly calls I had heard on the banks of the Naka River and in the park outside Meiji Shrine were voiceless voices—they were definite, unwavering words of truth, whose contents my heart and soul could intuitively recognize through their vibrations. But the spirits I heard now sounded to me no different from human voices. It was like hearing people talk with my eyes shut. Sometimes the voices echoed in my head, while at other times they were heard in my chest. This made me feel as if they were living humans, souls, and spirits, rather than the existence of divinity itself. Consequently, I felt that I wanted to confirm their authenticity. Although I had offered my life to God, I sometimes wondered whether I should entrust my body to a group of souls and spirits which I thought might have human emotions. Whenever this thought occurred to me, the group from the spiritual world would quickly respond, saying, "Your physical self has already been entrusted to us. You are to transform into a divine being by passing through various trials and tests from here on. If you have any reservations about it, we will restore you to your former state. You will revert to being an ordinary member of society, and will cease to take part in this large-scale divine activity."

I had been living with the sole desire of working for my country and for humanity, and had formed the opinion that this could not be achieved with ordinary human wisdom. Now that I had come this far, I could not bear the thought of being deserted by the supra-realistic abilities that had come to me. Even if my guiding spirits were not divine messengers themselves, that would be fine. I could keep on living for the purpose of bringing peace to humanity, no matter what, for the rest of my life. If, in the worst case, it turned out that they were malevolent souls, then I would just have to struggle to overcome their mental powers to the very end. I resolved my dilemma thusly, and quietly awaited further instructions from my spiritual guides.

My full-scale training then began under the direction of the spirits working behind me, with my home as the base. The first order I received was to stop all thoughts that passed through my brain. To rid myself of all thoughts? What a preposterous demand! One can perhaps block out all else by concentrating on a single task, but how can a person spend the entire day without thinking anything? Since olden times, even great priests had suffered from their inability to attain this exalted state of *Kuu*.

My own assignment was all the more difficult since it was not limited simply to sessions of seated meditation. My guiding spirits were forcing me into this difficult, or rather, impossible task. Naturally, the assignment had not come from the wishes of my deceased younger brother or my departed close friend. It appeared to be the order of someone at the center of this particular spiritual group. His or her words held a dignity close to that of the divine communications I had received by the Naka River and in the park outside Meiji Shrine. They were uncompromising, not faltering in the least.

I did not know how to carry out the assignment, but

in my desperate condition, I had no alternative but to do as ordered. I recalled the lamentations of Jeremiah in the Old Testament. I wondered if I might end up like him, who ended his life in anguish and sorrow according to the orders of the Lord Jehovah. Was I taking a first step in this direction?

"Now we will begin. First, we will leave home," said the spiritual beings. I left home, putting on my only suit, which had long worn thin. I had no idea at all as to where I was going or what I would do. I was not even permitted to consider asking a question. The moment I started wondering where I was heading, I was told to return home immediately. When I obeyed the order, they told me to start out again. Walking straight ahead would soon bring me to the end of the street, forcing me to turn in one direction or another. I, of course, imagined that I would be required to turn either right or left. At my first sign of hesitation, they ordered me once again to head back to the starting point.

This time, I safely turned right, then left. "Am I heading for the station?" I thought. That was no good, of course, and I had to head home once more. After having failed many times, I at last reached the station. The distance from home to the station was about a kilometer, and it had taken over two hours. However, even this was unknown to me until a while later. At the time, I merely continued walking, staring into the sky, trying to stop all the thoughts that disturbed me as they incessantly sprang up.

April, with its gentle breezes, lightened the hearts of the people strolling in the streets. This was the season of cherry blossom viewing parties. Among the bright streams of people, I was walking around with a desperate look on my face. I only thought *Kuu, Kuu, Kuu, Kuu*. There was no earth under my feet, no town around me. The only thing that continued to exist was the goal of stopping all thoughts. I repeated this to myself, going back and forth. I felt neither sorrow nor worry. I had no spare energy for grieving or worrying. In my mind there was only *Kuu, Kuu, Kuu, Kuu*. I was not given a moment of rest or distraction from anything but the idea of *Kuu*.

Upon reaching the station, I wondered if I was going to buy a ticket or not. That again was the wrong thing to do. I tried two, three, four, and five times. Finally, the word 'Kanamachi' came out of my mouth. It was not my own voice. One of the spirits behind me had said it using my vocal chords. Where was I anyway? At that moment, I had no consciousness of self. My physical being was perfectly empty and was left to the free use of these guiding spirits.

I rode the train bound for Kanamachi, but passed it and found myself at the end of the line, at Matsudo. I remained on board, even after all the other passengers had gotten off. The train departed again with new passengers, this time for Ueno. It passed Kameari and Senju, but I was still seated, struggling with the thoughts that would frequently come out, keeping my eyes open but looking at nothing. Thus, I took several round trips between Matsudo and Ueno, under the persistent observation of the spirits. The pain and agony of being unable to think about anything was beyond words.

At dusk, the spirits finally released me from the train and I returned home, rubbing my tired back. But I could not talk at all with my family, for how can a person talk without thinking about anything? I skipped lunch and dinner that day and, after a long meditation, got a bit of rest that night.

My training in ceasing all thought continued every day after that, along with consistent fasting. As I obeyed the instructions of the guiding spirits, my travels covered the entire Tokyo area. I even went as far as Yokohama several times. I secretly purified each house I walked by. Thought waves from the houses on either side of me would occasionally beckon to stop me, so that I would sometimes totter towards the right or the left. It is interesting that I got away with riding the private Keisei, Tobu, and Tamaden lines, along with various subway lines, with only a ticket for the shortest section of the public-owned Japan Railways. At any rate, my body was absent of thought waves, and did not belong to this world.

On another day, in a town called K, I was asked to pray for the turn of fortune of a certain household. While I prayed, an enormous swarm of emotional souls (normally referred to in Japan as 'wild fox spirits') suddenly attacked me. These souls had been connected with troubles in the family's traditional business. Although I was startled for a moment, the training I had been undergoing soon enabled me to restore the condition of 'no-thought,' and I resumed focusing solely on God. Throngs of souls continued to attack me, one after another. If I relaxed my attention for even a fraction of a second, it felt as though my body was about to be flailed in all directions. Then, when I again stabilized my concentration on God, I began to feel violently dizzy. I felt as if my whole brain were about to crumble, starting from right behind my eyes.

When I felt almost ready to collapse, the words of the spirits behind me flashed through my mind: "Think no thoughts." I then composed myself and continued to focus on God. After an hour of excruciating struggle, I felt that my heart had become perfectly pure and calm. The great throng of emotional souls had utterly vanished. Their emotions had been completely purified. This was a clear demonstration of the effectiveness of my discipline of stopping all thought. The struggle I had gone through was like a real death match, for had I succumbed to fear, I would have died on the spot or else gone genuinely mad. At that time I clearly understood through living experience that the greatest power we can use in the face of negatively-powered beings in unseen worlds is the firm faith to keep thinking of God, and the discipline to reject any kind of fear.

One day, I was walking slowly in the rain and wind. Large drops of rain came dripping from my hair and drenched my clothing. The rain had gradually soaked through to my chest and back, and my leather shoes, which already had several gaping holes in them, were saturated and weighed heavily on my feet. But I could not make haste, nor did I attempt to. Neither rain nor wind existed in my mind. I no longer felt even my own body. I was not moving of my own volition, nor was my behavior that of a sleepwalker or someone lost in thought. My soul's consciousness existed immovably at a point within *Kuu*. *Kuu, Kuu, Kuu, Kuu*, I thought.

Without a doubt, my true self firmly existed in a far distant place within the fathomless expanse of *Kuu*. But although I could clearly recognize its existence, I still could not reach this place. As I was steadily extinguishing all kinds of thoughts, my consciousness did not reside in my physical body; it was somewhere between my physical body and my true self. On the same plane as my own self-

159

awareness, I could also sense the consciousness of several spirits among the group that was acting upon my physical body. I had already transcended the wind and rain. As my body was being pelted by the wind and rain, my consciousness was intently ascending through the world of spirits and souls that exists beyond the wind and the rain.

I was later informed that the instruction to stop my thoughts had been the command of my guardian divinity, conveyed to me via the spirits working behind me, for the purpose of uniting my phenomenal self[28] with my true self. During this training period, I was posed many questions and given many tests by the spirits. Let me describe just a few of these.

One example was a battle I took on with complete terror. One night, while I was walking through various neighborhoods as usual, purifying the thought waves that had accumulated there, I suddenly heard the following words: "You will pass away within the next half hour. There is no way you can carry out the work of a bodhisattva[29] in this world, given your poor performance up to now. Prepare to ascend. You are out of time! Any second now, you will ascend! Ascend!" These words were repeated again and again, as if to mesmerize me. With them poured in a feeling of terror. The attack of the emotional souls I had encountered earlier could hardly be compared to this. Cornered by fear, I stood still on the spot. My body was bathed in a cold sweat. "It's time to ascend. There is no time left. Very soon, you will be in the next world." The words assailed me harder and harder.

When I was on the verge of despair, I spontaneously directed my mind to God. "God, God, God!" I shouted in desperation. Luckily, having long since become accustomed to practicing divine oneness, I instantly began to unite with God. Then, one part of the curtain of terror that hung in front of me began to lift.

At that moment, somewhere within my head, someone whispered to me, "The silent call."

No sooner had I heard this than I began to intone the silent call, "O—m," with all my might. The fear suddenly evaporated and light spread through my heart.

For some time after that, I believed that this had been a test from the devil, but I learned later that it was another hurdle placed before me by my guiding spirits. The advice to use the silent call seems to have been a spontaneous word of assistance from my brother in the spiritual world, who could not bear to see me in such agony.

On another day, the spirits said to me, "We know that you are finding it hard to live without money. Get off at Hamamatsuchō station. On your right hand side, you will find a woman of about forty selling public lottery tickets. Buy one from her bearing such and such a number."

I did not know if this advice was true or false, but I was indeed truly destitute. With the cost of daily train fares, I did not have even a penny left over to help my mother to buy food, even though I was traveling all around, practicing purifications, and attending gatherings at the Seicho-No-Ie center as well. I had decided to fast, so as not to put any additional burden on my mother. If I quit eating, the household expenses would be that much smaller, I figured, thinking, "God will surely do something to help, sooner or later."

It was under these circumstances that the spiritual advice about the lottery ticket was given to me. But I was not careless enough to be deceived by these words, as I was becoming somewhat accustomed to the discipline of stopping all thoughts. I headed for Hamamatsuchō station, reciting *Kuu, Kuu, Kuu* in my mind, as usual. Everything went as predicted. I would have failed this test, however, had I fallen into the belief that I was going to draw a winning number. Rather, I kept my mind free from all thoughts. I keenly remembered the saying: "A hundred pieces of knowledge cannot match a single deed of truth," and I strongly felt that putting everything into practice was the only thing that mattered. Whether I was to win at the lottery or not would be revealed to me later.

I bought the ticket bearing the designated number

from the woman, as foretold. But this indeed proved to be a test: the chosen number failed to come up.

At the time, I could sense that the spirits working behind me were observing every movement of my mind, and I calmly waited for their next words. I received no directions, but my feet naturally started to carry me in the direction of the Tamachi district of Tokyo. Before long, I found myself near the entrance of the University of C, located in a place called Sannohashi. Ms. M had recently taken a job there.

Now accustomed to thinking nothing at all, I stood near the gate and silently waited for the next instructions. The guiding spirits carried my feet to the reception desk without giving any instructions. It was at this instant that Ms. M came out, just as if she had been called. "Oh, this is a surprise. What brings you here today?" she asked.

"I happened to be in the neighborhood, so I thought I would drop by."

"Would you wait a moment while I get my things? It's Saturday and I was just leaving." Saying this, she left the room, hastily returning about five minutes later.

The two of us left together. It was a June day, well before dusk, and the town was still bright with sunlight. My threadbare summer clothes and worn out shoes, coming apart at the seams, could be plainly seen in the summer light. "You have gotten so thin since I saw you last," she said. "Why, you look ill. What's made you lose so much weight?"

"Well, I'm undergoing some training, and I've been fasting as well."

"You've got to take care of your health..." Saying this, Ms. M turned away from me, as though she could not bear to see how miserably thin and worn down I had become. It was only natural that she should be surprised by the drastic change in me, since we had communicated only through letters for nearly two months.

People in the neighborhood and friends of mine who had seen me walking around would say, "That young Masahisa, the son of Mr. Goi, is behaving very strangely, poor thing. He seems to have lost his wits. It's so sad. He was always such a good boy." They would even take the trouble of visiting my mother to express their concerns about me. With growing anxiety, my mother also attempted to have me change my ways. But she was totally at a loss. Her son had given up eating and scarcely said a word. When he did talk, he would come out with something bizarre. Nevertheless, he did not cause any trouble to others, nor did he show any signs of so-called 'insanity.' On the contrary, he had healed quite a number of sick people.

And so, my mother had half given up on me, as if I had already passed away, and permitted me to do as I wished. Still, it is easy to imagine how worried she must have been.

Ms. M must also have been pained at the changes in me. That day in June, the two of us rather spontaneously decided to go to Meiji Shrine, and we rode the train as far as Yoyogi station. As we stepped onto the grounds of the shrine, I suddenly exclaimed, "Oh, it's the Emperor Meiji! The Emperor is up in the blue sky! Bow your head, Ms. M, bow!" As I spoke, I inclined my head deeply. Following my example, Ms. M also bowed her head deeply. Passersby looked at us with a puzzled expression.

Her face flushed with a mixture of embarrassment and sorrow, Ms. M could hardly hold back the tears as she watched me gesturing toward the illusion in the empty sky. "He has finally gone mad. He has really lost his sanity," she seemed to be thinking.

"Let's go in," I said, walking with my eyes fixed on the heavens, oblivious to her grief. She seemed to be choked with pain, but followed me feebly, still sobbing.

After we paid our respects at the shrine, Ms. M finally stopped weeping and said, as if to cheer herself up, "I've taken up French."

"French? Of course, French!" No sooner had I said this than perfectly accented French-like words began to stream out of me. She gazed at me in astonishment. "How is that for French?" I asked.

"Oh, I've never heard any French like that," she said. And she again began to weep.

I later understood that these two incidents were trials formulated by the spirits at work behind me to measure the depth of Ms. M's love. Overwhelmed with grief, Ms. M kept weeping until we bid farewell, but she slipped a one thousand yen note[30] into my pocket before we parted. Although I had entrusted all my behavior to my guiding spirits, I said with my own words, in spite of myself, "Thank you, Ms. M, thank you."

Again, I reflected on the situation I found myself in. Having for the past four months entrusted all my physical actions to the spirits working behind me (whether they were angels or not was still unclear), I had borne up under rigorous trials from day to day, supported by my belief that my departed best friend and my brother Goro were working in the spiritual world behind me. Just this one time, however, I heartily wished that I could return to my old, usual self. I was filled with a wave of envy for all those normal people who had the free command of their own physical being and could strive for what they believed in, in their own ways and with their own will.

As if she had already guessed what was going on in my mind, Ms. M turned to me and said: "No matter what happens in the future, I will go with you. I will not leave you, even if you go raving mad. I will work, even if you don't bring in a cent. Please don't worry. Let's be patient. I am sure God will answer our pure-minded prayers." At that moment, her mind was made up. An intensely warm feeling began to well up from deep within my chest, and I stood stock still, overcome by profound emotion.

Approaching Perfect
Spiritual Freedom

I continued to be put through various trials and ordeals, one after another. This time, the spirits began to ask me a variety of questions inside my head.

"What is a human being?"

"A human being is a spirit that branches out from God."

"What is God?"

"God is the great life that fills the universe; it is the principle of life as well."

"What is meant by the great life?"

"It is all that lives, and all that is."

"What is all that is?"

They fired questions at me, one after another. If I didn't answer right away, I felt a band of pain tighten around my head, as if a bell were clanging violently inside it. My face quickly became suffused with blood. "I don't know," I said, unable to endure the pain.

"It is not that you don't know. You just cannot express it in human words. You already know the answer." Come to think of it, I did feel that I knew the answer deep in my mind. I realized that being unable to say something is different from not knowing it.

"Now, the next question. Why are humans born as physical beings?"

"It is to activate the divine principle of creation on the earthly plane."

"Good. By the way, where do you get these answers from?" I did not have even a moment to think about how to answer these questions. If I did not reply immediately, there was a sharp tightening of the pressure around my head. Physical pain was applied whenever my answer was not an instant echo to their question.

"I get them from my true being," I replied after hesitating for a moment and instantly feeling a tightening of the band of pain around my head.

"Is the true being you talk about the God of the universe?"

"It is the God of the universe, and it is also my true self."

"Do you mean to say that your true self is the God of

the universe?"

"It is the principle of creation, and one of the principles of the life of the universal God."

"What is your physical body?"

"It is a vessel that houses my true self."

"Where does your individual self reside?"

"It resides in my subconscious and physical embodiments."

"Is the individual self the same as God?"

"It is a being of cause and effect, but it contains God within it."

"Are you then a being of cause and effect?"

"I am a ray of divine life that is on the point of freeing itself from karmic causes and effects."

"What kind of person was Buddha?"[31]

"He was an enlightened person who became free from the law of causality and achieved oneness with his divine self."

"Do you think you can be like Buddha?"

"My true being knows the answer."

"Was Buddha also instructed, and did he learn things within his head, as you are doing now?"

"I do not think such a thing happened to him after he attained his awakening. I think his divine self worked directly through his physical being in all matters."

"What was the case with Jesus Christ?"

"I think it was the same."

"Why was such a great person crucified?"

"The Christ was not crucified. What was crucified was merely the physical body, the vessel that contained the Christ." This answer seemed to have impressed the spirits, as I felt waves of their approval being directed toward me. My heart was perfectly pure and transparent, and I clearly observed that no thoughts from my individual ego remained in my brain. I felt as if my divine and physical selves had become perfectly fused in a straight line connecting heaven and earth. Whatever problem or question might be put before me, I felt that I would be able to answer it.

The queries from the spirits continued. "How can the human world be delivered from its suffering and agony?"

"By our letting people know of human truth and divine concepts."

"How do you inform them of these things?"

"That is the question I have been struggling with. I think it is important to spread books of truth as quickly and as widely as possible."

"Can people be awakened just by reading books?"

"This is the biggest question that confronts me. In my present state of mind, I do not yet have a clear answer to it."

"You said your answers came from your true being. Isn't the answer known to your true being?"

"My true being knows it, but my physical brain is not trained enough to express my own answer in words. That may take time."

"What other means are there aside from books?"

"There is prayer. A prayer that resonates from our inner divine source will purify all the karma of this world."

"Will such violent karmic waves be purified so easily?"

"I do not think it can be done easily, but I do not know another means that works better than prayer."

"The materialists would laugh if they heard you say such a thing."

"Everyone might laugh at me at first. But that kind of laughter is only a manifestation of karma, so it will gradually be purified as a first step."

"How are you going to go about praying?"

"Thanks to the training I have gone through thus far, I have become fairly well disassociated from my individual ego, and I feel that I can readily entrust everything to God. My prayer will be a declaration of complete entrustment to the divine, and of letting my divine embodiment carry the responsibility for the future of the human world."

"How will you impart true principles to others?"

"I will explain that our true selves are not confined

to our physical existence, but work freely throughout the universe. Then, I will ask people to pray for world peace as if they are proclaiming it from the source of their being, rather than timidly begging for it with their physical karmic thoughts. This attitude is important, because anxiety and fear are hindrances to prayer."

"It sounds pretty hard. Few people will join you with such a difficult teaching. The general public would rather follow someone who offers answers to their actual, specific problems, like the Communists do."

"I used to think so, too. I wished for super-human powers that would improve the world all at once. Now, thanks to the training you have given me, I have been able to exhibit this kind of power. However, even if I could train myself to where I could exert the same mystical powers as Buddha, I do not think that it would make this world improve right away. I feel that a certain amount of time and effort will be needed before we can bring large numbers of people into the spirit of true prayer. In the meantime, Japan and other parts of the world may fall under the rule of the Soviet Union, with its calls for human equality in a communist-based society. However, human beings will not let their lives be dictated by this sort of ideology for a long time, because it stems from a materialistic philosophy, and does not hold the power to purify the karma of this world. On the other hand, our prayer will never grow obsolete, no matter what other ideas or philosophies may appear, or what other measures may be taken. Until human souls are purified and returned to their original, divine consciousness, a truly peaceful world will never be revealed."

"What would you do if the Earth were to perish in the meantime, due to war and natural disasters?"

"For us who know or are striving to know the divine reality of our true being, it would matter little if the Earth perished. However, since the existence of God is infinite love itself, I believe God will refrain from giving such immense terror to human beings. Otherwise, there would be no reason for divine and spiritual beings like you to guide me in this way, just for my own sake. Now, having come to this point, I can really understand, with my whole body and soul, what Jesus Christ meant when he uttered the words: *Thy will be done.*"[32]

"That is all for the questions. You will experience something different tomorrow night."

That was the end of the questions posed by my guiding spirits. To me, all their words had sounded exactly as if I were hearing human voices. From then on, however, none of these voices, automatic writings, or bizarre instructions from the spiritual world would ever again intrude into my physical being. My training in stopping all thoughts had succeeded at last, and I became free from the habit of thinking. Yet, I could talk and move my hands, my legs, and my whole body whenever necessary.

My individual physical consciousness no longer existed in this world, because I had returned to heaven all the thoughts I had conceived throughout my past and present lifetimes. My being was perfectly free and clear. I only existed there, silently and stably, bridging heaven and earth. I intuitively felt that my individual self, which had been suspended for such a long time, had already been reunited with my infinite, divine self. This feeling was proven true the following night.

Heaven and Earth
Become One

That night, as usual, I meditated before going to bed. My training in stopping all thoughts enabled me to immediately enter the condition of oneness with my divine self.

No sooner had I started to meditate than I stopped inhaling entirely; my breath simply continued to flow outward. Right in front of me there appeared a thick crystalline pillar that looked as if it reached straight to heaven. I began to ascend the pillar, riding, as it were, on my own exhalation. Rising, I saw layers of grey clouds slightly tinged with yellow that appeared to be a borderline between the worlds above and below. Passing through it without any strain, I found myself among layers of pure white clouds, which I also went through without effort. After passing through strata of light-filled clouds in shades of blue, green, and bluish- and reddish-purple, I finally emerged from the seventh layer, a spiritual world of radiant gold. I then discovered myself in a world of absolute brilliance which could only be described as a refined synthesis of all color. There, I observed myself, seated in a shining, golden chair and wearing a purple hat similar to those worn by aristocrats in olden times. Before I could think anything at all, my consciousness merged into this celestial self. Then I—that is, my newly united self—stood up quietly.

Even as I sat meditating in my mother's house, meditating in my mother's house, I had indeed entered the divine world. I could see various divinities moving back and forth. I perceived a mountain resembling Mount Fuji and a river of abundant water. I could even see a building that resembled the Ryūgū Palace.[33] All kinds of light flowed incessantly toward and away from me, moving in all directions—upwards, downwards, right to left, and left to right. The wondrous thing about it was that all these sights became visible to me, one after another, as I remained firmly rooted in one spot. I was now confirming the reality of what had happened. My true, divine self, which exists throughout the universe, had become united with my individual, earthly self. What I had already sensed spiritually was now becoming clearly recognizable in my individual consciousness.

During my training in the stopping of thoughts, I had always been aware of the existence of my true being, somewhere above me, just out of reach. Yet, I had been unable to attain oneness with it. Now, having reached this state of oneness, an enormous inner light burst forth, nullifying all obstacles. Ever since that time, I have felt that I am light itself, and by emitting my inner light, I have been enlivening those who are sad or afflicted and harmonizing those who are suffering from illness.

Now, I also clearly recognize that 'heaven' refers to the realm that is the interior part of a human being, and that the 'divine self' is none other than the selfless light existing in our innermost depths. In performing one action of truth, I was at last able to surpass a hundred pieces of knowledge, enabling me to directly perceive the totality of my true being.

Having ascended to heaven is the same as having plunged into the profundity within. Explained from a spatial point of view, I had merged with my celestial embodiment; explained from the point of view of awareness, I had returned to my original, divine consciousness.

The time it took me to undergo this whole process measured about thirty minutes in this phenomenal world. I realized that *Kuu* itself was not the ultimate aim of my training in stopping all thoughts. To exist in *Kuu* means to wholly extinguish all worldly, phenomenal thoughts. The moment one has attained *Kuu*, the essential world and the essential self unite with the phenomenal world and the phenomenal self, giving birth to a unified self encompassing heaven and earth and comprising both the physical and the divine consciousness.

What is the true, essential self? The true self is the divine self, filled with merciful love, harmony, and perfect spiritual freedom. The saint known as Sakyamuni Buddha was able to manifest his true self perfectly. His theoretical explanations were perfect and complete, and he also manifested perfect and complete love. On top of that, he had the ability to exert perfect spiritual and mystical power.

Theory alone, no matter how perfect, does not make a person a great saint. Nor does having spiritual and mystical power, no matter how superb. Even one who possesses both of these will not necessarily be called a Buddha. For, unless everything about oneself springs from a mind of perfect, all-encompassing love, one cannot carry out a central role in uplifting humanity from its misery and confusion. In order to freely extinguish the karma of this world, the centralmost figure needs to have perfectly developed theoretical teachings and mystical powers which are at all times sustained and guided by the absolute existence of love. In thinking of this, I am once again overcome with feelings of fathomless awe and respect for the greatness of Sakyamuni Buddha.

Sakyamuni, whom I have long looked up to as my uniquely respected teacher, appeared to me while I was meditating the following morning. Shortly after I began to meditate, a brilliant light, unlike anything I had ever seen before, began to shine in front of my eyes. I gazed intently at this light without thinking anything. Then, the form of Buddha, seated with his legs crossed on a pure white lotus flower and looking exactly as he did in his carved statues, descended from far, far above. He extended his arms toward me. Without thinking anything, I extended my arms toward him. Into my outstretched palms, he placed a round golden stone that appeared to be the *Nyoi-hōju*.[34] I received the sphere and placed it in the bosom of my spiritual body. He then gave me a slightly smaller sphere of brilliant gold, which I also accepted and put in my bosom. After that, he gave me five leaves that looked like *sakaki*,[35] and he disappeared into the midst of the brilliance. As I was meditating to bid him farewell, out of the same glorious light appeared Jesus Christ, a golden cross on his back. In the same instant, the Christ rushed straight into me, merging with my whole body. As he disappeared, I heard a strong voice proclaim, "Thou art one with Christ."

My meditation that morning ended with that voice echoing in my ears. What I felt after that was not so much a deep emotion as a profound sense of mission that resonated intently from the bottom of my chest, like a splitting pain. My soul clearly knew that what had occurred was not imaginary, because I felt an inner voice that said, "You are perfectly free from this day forward. Go and accomplish your mission." I had become a spiritually awakened person who directly knows and perceives everything by means of intuition.

After that day, in all ways, I returned to the appearance and outward behavior of my former self, before I became engrossed in things like souls and spirits. I again thought about everything with my own mind, spoke entirely with my own words, moved my own hands and legs, and faced everyone with my own smile. My eyes no longer gazed at the open sky, and my mild expression freely revealed the emotions that arose in my heart. I no longer called out to God, or pressed others to listen to me talk about spiritual matters. For my parents, my older brother and his wife, and my younger brother, their beloved Masahisa had come alive again. Every night, their gentle, thoughtful, easy-going and cheerful son would massage his father's sore legs and his mother's stiff shoulders.

Occasionally, as I massaged her shoulders, my mother would start talking about her deceased son. "I wonder what has happened to Goro," she would say.

And I would answer casually, "Goro is with me. He is hard at work."

The other day, my mother confessed, "I'm so happy to see that you're better. It was terrible, the past few months. The neighbors used to come and talk to me about you, and I was really concerned. Still, I knew that a good boy like you would never go wrong, especially the way you trusted in God and always thought about others and what you could do for them. I was sure that you would not go off the deep end. Toshio and Susumu (my younger brothers) believed in you, too."

Smiling happily, I continued to rub her shoulders. To this frail old lady with her spare frame and rounded back, I owed more than to anyone else in the world. My mother kept on working for her children seriously and honestly, never sparing the slightest effort. Perhaps it was simply her ardent love and affection for her children that gave her the strength to always keep working despite the fragile condition of her body, which now weighed less than 40 kilograms (88 pounds).

Once I had manifested my true self, an increasing number of visitors came to my humble home, keeping me busy with consultations on life, or with healing the afflicted. This, combined with the fact that I no longer refused their offerings, was sufficient to revive my mother's strength.

My other great benefactor in this world was my father. Due to poor health, he retired from work at an early age, but in his later years he put great spiritual trust in me. He was always eager to hear my talks, and several times I was moved to tears to see him following my advice by meditating in front of the *Kannon* statuette. Thanks to his receptiveness to divine love, when he died in January 1954, he easily ascended to the spiritual world enveloped in my light. He is now working with me happily and vividly, as a valued aide in my work.

During my lifetime, I studied a variety of spiritual teachings. Finally, after going through my own direct spiritual experiences under the guidance of my guardian divinity, I reached a perfectly free state of mind, and all my actions sprang directly from my radiant, true self. Acting as such, I have made a full-fledged step toward the attainment of my mission on earth. As I reflect on it now, I am amazed at how I could have endured the excruciating spiritual disciplines that were given to me. There seem to have been two power sources that sustained me. One was the sense of assurance I received from the presence of my best friend and my younger brother, who were always supporting me from behind. The other was my unshakable belief in the love that I felt for other people and for my country, along with a fathomless longing for the great harmony of all human beings.

On many occasions, I was driven just one step short of either insanity or an agonizing death. What finally rescued me was the power of my belief in myself and my absolute faith in divine love. Had I entertained any selfish desire for supernatural powers, I certainly could not have become as I am today. When people face their own death, without exception, they see all their past thoughts and deeds passing before them, as in a kaleidoscope. As long as one wishes for spiritual powers for self-serving reasons, one will never be spiritually awakened in the true sense. This is because it is impossible to ascend to high spiritual and divine planes while riding on the low thought waves of egocentric desires.

In those planes, there are immovable laws and clearly defined phases of development, and being able to relinquish one's egocentric desires has a great deal to do with the degree of a person's spiritual awakening. Likewise, if one disciplines oneself out of a desire to be superior to others, to show off in front of others, or to attain social status, financial benefit, and the like, one will attract the intervention of creatures in the subconscious realm who hold the same kinds of desires. These creatures, who know nothing of a human being's innate divinity, or of the principles and objectives of the divine will, often present themselves in the guise of divine guides, and offer sporadic predictions and perform healing feats which are beyond the capabilities of ordinary people.

Once people have asked for the assistance of these

deluded souls, they become elated and puffed up with pride because of what they can achieve without making use of their own abilities. Such people end up lacking in diligence, sincerity, and the free will necessary to live with dignity in the human world. Even worse, they deprive others of their free will, contributing as much, if not more, to the destruction of this world as do those who deny divinity or concern themselves only with the material realm. Although at first glance, it may appear to be of little significance, this kind of behavior displays a spiritual ignorance of the most lamentable and dangerous kind.

Since I am well aware of this danger through my own experience, I caution people not to fall into the trap of idly wishing for psychic abilities. I explain it to them this way: "Because you have your guardian spirits (enlightened ancestors) and guardian divinities with you at all times, guiding you and protecting you from harm, it would be good if you could direct your thoughts to them in all that you do. If you keep asking for their assistance, you will naturally acquire correct psychic abilities if they are necessary for you." I also mention that if there is any kind of danger coming your way, your spiritual and divine protectors are always working to guide you away from it in some manner or other. I can say this with absolute certainty because, upon finishing my own disciplines, I became clearly aware that my guardian divinity and spirits had been watching over me from directly behind, since before the time of my birth.

Had I known from the start what I am now conveying to others, I might have attained my present state earlier and with less discomfort. As it happened, though, there was no other choice, because it was one of my missions in life to let other people know about the experiences I went through in reaching my own awakening. Because those experiences enabled me to provide guidance to others, their purpose encompasses future generations. Of course, terms like 'guardian divinities' and 'guardian spirits' have been employed since olden times, but their existence has not previously been explained in such clear and practical terms as I am doing now, enabling people to more easily connect with them and attain a firmer grasp of the truth. I know full well that the intention of the universal God can never be realized on Earth without the aid of our guardian spirits and divinities.

One of the manifestations of the universal God is God as the universal law. Being without thought, form, or emotion, the law exists as the eternal flow of great life, within which streams each smaller, human life. When these smaller lives first came into being, ethereal substance was formed, and then physical embodiments described as 'material substance' came into being for the first time. These smaller lives, branching out from the great life, began to reside within individually distinct subconscious and physical embodiments.[36] At that time, there arose a sense of one individual life being separate from another. This sense of separateness gave rise to the physical instincts of self-protection, which in turn generated a variety of self-centered desires. This led to the activity of karma, and a karmic realm took shape.

If this world were ruled by divine law alone, it would inevitably have perished amidst the whirlpools of karma. This conclusion can be reached by anyone who is able to observe this world objectively. Divine law is without thought, form, or emotion, for if the law had emotions, it would no longer be the law. And so, it follows that what is without thought or emotion does not think of rescuing humanity from the activity of karma.

A seed that is sown bears its own fruit. This is a law. Therefore, if one sows resentment, waves of resentment return again to oneself. If one sows anger, it engenders further anger, which eventually returns to oneself. And if one sows sorrow, sorrow returns to oneself. This is a law, but this law itself does not hold the means for uplifting humanity from its misery. Atheistic theory is rooted in this law. If the human world were governed only by divine law, it would be a world conforming to materialistic principles, a world where the weak fall prey to the strong, and the Earth's destruction would be merely a matter of time.

The 'God' expressed in the words 'God is love' is not God as divine law, but God as our guardian divinities. It is not the all-inclusive divine life which fills the universe, but a divine entity which has the same feelings of merciful love as human beings have. The reason why, practically speaking, a contradiction has been created in some religious theories is that these two aspects of God have been mixed together as one.

No matter how fervently we may ask the universal law to grant our requests, there is no reason to expect that this will be done. This is because law itself can never be bent. Therefore, until we live in tune with the universal law, we will never attain lasting happiness. And, once we become derailed from the universal law, it is next to impossible for us to return to the law by ourselves. If we could do it on our own, no one would ever feel any need for religion, or to call upon God.

It is at this point that religions concerned wholly with worldly gains have been able to slip in and take advantage of people. Such organizations disregard what truly benefits people—the purification of the soul—and instead encourage their members to seek only short-term advantages. How much a person may suffer later on as a result is not considered. However, the people who rely on these religions care only about their immediate problems. If they can somehow get beyond their present discomfort, it seems like a great blessing for them. This, I think, is why our societies are inundated with profit-seeking religions.

The cause of this phenomenon is that, in many cases, the scrupulous religions expound their theories without taking note of the contradiction mentioned above. No matter how correct their theory may appear to be, if it is a theory of divine law alone, and does not impart a feeling of deep, merciful love, then people will naturally turn to religions promising bigger worldly gains, even though those religions may be predatory ones.

Having witnessed these two currents in today's religions, I place emphasis on the guidance and powerful saving grace of our guardian divinities, who are the existence of divine love, as well as on correct spiritual theory (for further discussion on this subject, please see my book *God and Man*). In doing so, the liberating power of our guardian divinities and spirits becomes my focal point, and I treat all instances of karmic cause and effect as remnants of the now-vanishing past.

Even if one declares that there is perfect harmony in our essential divine condition, one corrupts this teaching when one applies the law of mind to actual phenomena. Moreover, for many people, the unseen, intangible God seems too vague for them to grasp, or to fully place their trust in, no matter how hard they may pray. This is why people seek to be uplifted by a holy being who has actually lived in the physical world, such as Jesus or Mary, as a personification of divine love.

In Buddhism, the doctrines alone are too abstruse for the general population to understand. Therefore, people make statues of the Buddha in an effort to absorb an uplifting power through them. The same applies to the Buddhist sutras. Regardless of whether they understand them or not, the majority of people chant them simply because they believe them to be precious and powerful words which impart sacred blessings. In other words, people would rather rely on someone or something tangible to encourage and console them.

Religious theory alone, if it disregards this common feature of human psychology, is no match for the predatory religions which entice people with the promise of worldly gains. The majority of people wish to find happiness immediately, in their daily lives. They do not mind setting aside eternal spiritual freedom for another day if they can have a God who will deftly extract them from their present-day, real-life problems.

Nor is just talking about guardian divinities and spirits sufficient to give people a real sense of how close they are to us. People need to feel that their guardian divinities and spirits have the same loving emotions as humans do.

Additionally, it is helpful for people to know that these protective beings are their own powerful, enlightened ancestors, or divinities who have been taking exclusive care of them since before they were born in this world.

People need a parental divine love which will attend to them above all else, no matter what happens. I point to the existence of these kinds of guardian divinities, and I also explain that our guardian spirits are working under the guardian divinities' direction. I assist people in distinctly recognizing their guardian spirits' existence by explaining that they are truly our own ancestors who existed far, far back in our own family lineage. In this way, I break through the vague, abstract notions previously held of guardian divinities and spirits, and show them to be warmhearted, loving, familiar beings whom each person can embrace as his or her own.

I say to people, "If you continuously thank your guardian divinity and spirits and entrust yourself completely to them, this will make it easier for them to lift away the smudges and stains that cloud your heart. At the same time, they will always be able to shield you from danger." This kind of teaching makes it very easy for people to practice complete entrustment to God. Actually, the truth of the matter is that the enormous work being done by our guardian divinities and spirits in the divine and spiritual worlds, both for individuals and all of humanity, is far beyond the imagination. I can say this with absolute certainty because I have placed my physical being at the disposal of those divinities and spirits, as a place where they can carry out their purifying activities.

If you offer people a teaching that aims at correcting their attitudes and actions without alleviating their anxieties and fears, it only enables them to bear up and persevere at a particular time and place. It does not really dispel their habitual, self-restricting thoughts and emotions (their karma). Any kind of theory, no matter how noble, can be difficult to practice in one's emotions and actions, even if one understands it with one's intellect. Not only that, such theoretical knowledge can even have a detrimental effect when people use it to blame and judge themselves, turning themselves into well-intentioned people who do not live up to their full potential.

In order to uplift people and free them from their miseries, the first priority is to remove their daily fears and anxieties. This does not mean that we should simply say, "Don't worry, everything will be all right," to someone whose problem has not been solved, simply in order to console the person. It is not enough to put a person's mind at ease with words alone. It is also useless to pretend that we can do something we cannot do. Instead, we must show the person a way to achieve peace of mind that can be practiced with the emotions as well as with actions.

To do this, it is most important to instill people with the assurance that each of us is always protected by God. In addition, the method must be one which people can practice without strain, and which will correctly guide them toward the way of love and truth.

With all this in mind, I have re-expressed commonly used spiritual terms such as 'cause and effect' and Seicho-No-Ie's horizontal principle of the 'law of mind' in ways that may release people from their anguish, saying: "The evils and misfortunes that appear in your life are nothing to be afraid of, since they are the vanishing shapes of your past mistaken thoughts and actions, emerging now in order to disappear forever. Once they have disappeared, your soul will certainly be that much more purified. This will open up a happier future for you. So, please do not accuse yourself on account of your previous thoughts and actions. Constantly remind yourself: 'Oh! Thanks to this present circumstance, some sort of unharmonious element (karma) from my past thoughts and actions is now disappearing, so that the light of my inner soul will shine brighter and brighter, and I will soon have a truly happy life.'"

I suggest that people firmly and strongly encourage themselves in this way. At the same time, I also suggest that they direct their present thoughts to their guardian divinities and spirits with words and feelings like this:

"Dear guardian divinities and spirits, please purify and remove my karma as soon as possible, and guide me to accomplish my divine purpose in this world." In this way, I assist them in turning an incident or condition that appears to be unfortunate into a sign of something positive, so that their hearts will face in a bright and hopeful direction. To back this up, I refer to the principle of the 'law of mind,' which states that a bright heart invites a bright future, and a loving heart invites a love-filled world around us. In ways like these, I help people to instill only brightness at the bottom of their hearts.

As the basis for all this, I further explain the following truth, which I grasped through my own direct experience: "Your true being exists in the divine world as a sublime divine life, and in that plane you are working freely for humanity and the universe. The 'you' who works in the physical plane, within the 'container' known as your physical body, is a spirit branching out from God. So, please try your best not to create negative, dark thoughts that will interfere with your divine work, such as thinking of yourself or of other human beings as foolish, wicked, or worthless. If dark thoughts like these come to you, reject them immediately, again and again, seeing them as the now-disappearing reverberations of your previous karmic thoughts. Continue to pray intently, while affirming your own positive future and the forthcoming manifestation of great harmony among all human beings. If you keep doing this, your physical self and your free, divine self will, without a doubt, be perfectly unified some day, enabling you to attain a true, universal awareness. It is for this purpose that your guardian divinities and spirits have been accompanying you and purifying your karmic thoughts."

Human beings are, utterly and completely, individual manifestations of the one great universal God. They are like stars shining brightly in the great sky. The concepts and ideas emitting from the infinite mind of God are, in essence, already being revealed via the light and creative power of each individual human being. As time flows on, the universal divine mind will project itself more and more onto this earthly world. When it has fully projected itself, it will be the time when heaven becomes one with earth, and the divine reality becomes manifest on the physical plane.

When human beings, who are projections of the divine mind on Earth, concentrate wholeheartedly on their own assigned roles, all humanity will be able to see the manifestation of heaven on Earth without any pain or trouble. However, the physical human consciousness has, by now, wholly forgotten its original divine identity and its divine source. It has become enveloped in whirlpools of physically-oriented thoughts, which discriminate between one's own gains and losses and those of others. These karmic whirlpools are completely covering people, inhibiting the flow of divine light that shines deep within them.

Through my own experience, I was able to firmly catch hold of the brilliant heavenly light as it appeared for an instant from behind the whirling waves of human beings' thoughts. Under the protection of my guardian divinities and guardian spirits, I succeeded in attaining the state of *Kuu*, or freedom from all thought. I realized that fleeting emotions of elation, anger, sorrow, and pleasure are nothing more than vanishing waves of karmic cause and effect. From that moment on, my karmic self ceased to exist and, directly expressing my true self, I commenced my work as a bodhisattva. Presently, I am making use of my physical being to work in this world as one who unites heaven and earth.

The physical embodiments which human beings commonly think of as 'themselves' are not really their true selves. They are shapes formed by their past thought waves. Seen from the viewpoint of our true, essential selves, our physical selves are without lasting substance. They are like bubbles on the surface of the ocean, or castles built on the sand, which appear and disappear with each passing moment. For as long as people keep clutching only at these kinds of evanescent forms and shapes, no matter how they may talk about world peace or human happiness, it will never bring any lasting results. I can say this clearly, with absolute certainty. Until human beings free themselves once and for all from their past ways of thinking, and directly illuminate the world with the divine light which radiates from deep within their original being,[37] the divine plane (the realm of heaven) will not reveal itself on Earth.

This is why I keep explaining to people that their true, essential self is constantly emitting light, and that the karmic fluctuations that are perceived by the five senses are impermanent manifestations that appear in the process of fading away. My role is to help all people clearly recognize, as quickly as possible, that converting their physical embodiments from containers of karmic thoughts into vessels of light and divinity is the way to freedom for both themselves and all humanity.

My newly born self does not think things out with my physical brain. Nor do I collect and store up my thoughts. I speak and move my hands and legs naturally, without thinking about it. Everything I say, whether speaking about truth or just chatting and joking, is expressed naturally and spontaneously. Yet, none of my words or actions lacks normality or common sense. On the contrary, my behavior might even appear ordinary to an extreme. To people who have known me for a long time, I look like the same old Masahisa Goi, and my daily way of life is normality itself.

As normal as I seem, though, I reside in a completely different sphere from those who believe that a human being is simply a physical body. To explain it in plain terms, I move my physical body and speak physical words from a realm that exists independently of the physical world. This realm is, in other words, the realm transcending the egocentric emotions.[38] It is the divine realm that exists deep within the human mind, far beyond the world of thought waves. From that realm, or plane, my true self works through my physical being, using it as a vessel, or workplace.

Whenever people consult with me, my true self utilizes my physical entity and my past physical thoughts, in a way suitable for each person. And so, with the wisdom and light of my true, divine self, I offer guidance to each person who comes to see me, and I purify him or her. I now exist on Earth as a person returning from divine oneness.[39] I take on the worries and sorrows of others as my own. Placing myself in their situations, I offer guidance to people based on my direct spiritual awareness.

Even if one has become spiritually enlightened in some way, one cannot melt into oneness with the people who come to ask for advice if one always takes the standpoint of an 'enlightened person.' This is because one inevitably finds oneself looking down on others. In my case, when I meet with someone, everything about that person is projected into my mind, just as it is. And so, without the slightest need for skill or effort, I naturally place myself in the other person's position. When facing a child, I become a child. When facing an elderly person, or a husband, or a wife, in my heart, I too am an elderly person, husband, or wife. Once I have put myself entirely in the other person's place, I gradually uplift him or her to a higher state. This is my present way of guiding people. There are times when I find myself practicing roundabout maneuvers, or even telling little white lies, but these are always done out of love, for the sake of helping and guiding people.

What always moves me to tears when guiding different people are the painstaking efforts of their own guardian spirits, their enlightened ancestors. How hard these guardian spirits have been working, trying to protect their descendants who have been gradually drifting from the path of truth, dragged along by their past karmic thoughts. Since the work of these protective beings is hidden and cannot be perceived by the five senses, they are never thanked by anyone. They are like the pillars which sustain a house. At all times, never resting for a moment, they are expending every iota of their power and energy in an effort to come to the rescue of their descendent, and are absorbing enormous suffering on their descendant's behalf.

I keenly feel that if people are under the illusion that they are managing their entire lives with only their own power, they owe a big apology to their guardian spirits. How much lighter the burden of the guardian spirits would be if only human beings gave thanks to them! This, in turn, would allow people's futures to improve by leaps and bounds. If a person wishes to develop his or her spirituality, I strongly feel that the first and foremost thing to do is to live with gratitude to one's guardian spirits.

By July 1950, I was seldom at my parents' house, and stayed at various homes as I traveled, doing my work. My wife, who had at last won the consent of her family, came to marry me, bringing with her only a few personal belongings, which she carried with her. I was scheduled to give a talk that night in the town of Ichikawa. The venue for the talk was Shōnkaku, which later became our *dōjō*.[40] My wife, who had arrived just before the start of the lecture, sat beside me, her eyes to the ground. I greeted the audience, saying, "I would like you to meet my wife. Today is our wedding day." My wife bowed silently. That was our wedding ceremony, and the go-betweens were my guardian divinities.[41]

We were married at last, but we had no house to live in. Although I was not the least bit uneasy, it was not difficult to imagine how my wife was feeling. Such an odd man, once behaving as if he were almost insane, offering only an uncertain future, and not even a place to stay on their wedding night—this was the man she was going to call her husband for the rest of her life. It was not surprising that she should look sad.

However, at the end of the personal consultations that followed the lecture, the oft-spoken words of truth, that anything a person really needs will be given to him or her, were proven true. A man who was badly in need of money wanted to let the second floor of his house, and entreated me to aid him in finding a tenant. Although I did not have a cent on me, my wife happened to have brought with her the exact amount that the man needed. "God gives people what they need, when they need it." My whole way of life had been based on this principle, and this was a perfect example of it. It was eleven-thirty at night, and everything had come together at the last hour.

After my spiritual awakening, many mysterious stories were told to me. One person said that he felt as if his body were being lifted up to heaven when I prayed for him. Another said that when he closed his eyes, he saw a vision of me above the goddess of mercy, astride a dragon deity.

Shortly after my marriage, I dropped by the home of a certain Mr. Shimada who lived in the Hirata district of

Ichikawa. His oldest son, Shigemitsu, wanted to take my picture, so before I left, I let him take two photos of me in the house and one in front of the gate. In the two that were taken indoors, I was sitting Japanese style (on my knees, with my feet tucked behind me) and forming an *IN*.[42] When the photos were developed, in the background of one appeared the figure of the goddess of mercy and the face of a saintly-looking archaic gentleman wearing a crown. In the other photo there appeared a small figure of Sakyamuni Buddha sitting on a lotus flower. Then, in the one taken in front of the gate, in place of my physical body there was a sphere of light which was my spiritual body. I later learned that this phenomenon occasionally occurred with some advanced yogis. Many people who know me continue to keep copies of this photo with them like a talisman, as rare proof of the teaching that a human being's true body is not the physical one, but consists of pure light. The light waves emitting from this picture also have a special power to eliminate misfortune, and many people have told remarkable stories of how they have eluded accidents and disasters when carrying it.

It is difficult to live one's life with intellectual knowledge alone, since there are many things in this world that cannot be explained by the evidence perceived with the five senses. It is my firm belief that the mysterious power of the universe—the mystic door of wonders—will open first to those who can smoothly and naturally believe in God and perform deeds of love.

Human beings came from God, and everything in the universe is in the hands of God. If one truly wishes to lead a happy life, it is essential to first of all believe in God and know that one is not the mass of stiffened thought waves known as the physical body, but is one inseparable ray of everlasting, indestructible divine light.

How happy are those who simply believe in divine love.

How happy are those who live with actions of love and truth.

How happy are those who believe in the existence of the good and truthful guardian divinities and spirits who are at work behind all people.

How happy are those who can always thank their guardian divinities and spirits.

Heaven will be your dwelling place.

Notes

1. In the original, the author uses the term *konpaku* (魂魄), which refers to the activity of subconscious and physical elements combined.

2. *Tanka* (短歌) is a poem consisting of 31 Japanese syllables grouped in units of 5, 7, 5, 7, and 7. *Tanka* means 'short poem.' *Haiku* (俳句) is an even shorter poem, consisting of only 17 Japanese syllables.

3. Nerima is a district of Tokyo, located about ten miles northwest of Nihonbashi. In those days, it was a suburb of Tokyo.

4. Ieyasu Tokugawa (1542-1616) was the first leader of the Tokugawa Shogunate in Japan.

5. Referring to traditional Japanese poetry, called *waka* (和歌).

6. *Kuu* (空) is sometimes translated as 'stillness,' 'emptiness,' or 'nothingness.' Masahisa Goi explains: *Kuu is not a nihilistic or negative condition. It contains nothing, yet everything. It is the infiniteness of life itself, divinity itself, living vibrantly.*

7. Mushanokoji Saneatsu was born in Tokyo in 1855. He started a naturalist movement and created a utopian community in Miyazaki Prefecture, where he attempted to put his ideas into practice.

8. 'The attacks of Genkō' refers to two thirteenth century attacks on Japan which were thwarted because of strong winds.

9. *Shiatsu* (指圧) is a healing treatment involving the application of finger pressure to specific points which are considered energy centers in the human body.

10. *Hyaku Ji Nyoi* (百事如意) can be translated as 'Fulfill All Your Divine Intentions.'

11. Masaharu Taniguchi (1893-1985) was born in Kobe, Japan and founded the Seicho-No-Ie movement in 1930. He authored numerous books, including the *Truth of Life* series, and traveled throughout the world to communicate his teachings.

12. Seicho-No-Ie is a nondenominational movement founded in 1930 by Dr. Masaharu Taniguchi, based on the belief that all religions emanate from one universal God. It propagates the principle that every person is innately divine and possesses of all the creative powers of God.

13. *Sensei* (先生) is the Japanese word for 'teacher,' used to show respect for people who are considered wise, learned, or advanced in their field of work or study.

14. Tenri-kyō (天理教) is a spiritual faith of Shinto origin, founded in 1838 by Ms. Miki Nakayama.

15. Kurozumi-kyō (黒住教) is a spiritual faith founded in 1814 by the Shinto priest Munetada Kurozumi (1780-1850).

16. Shiba is the name of an area and also a park located in Minato Ward, in the center of Tokyo.

17. Tokuda, Shiga, and Yashiro Ii were prominent figures in the labor movements and social reforms of post-war Japan.

18. The reference for these words, which the author attributes to Jesus, is unknown.

19. The term used in Japanese is *ōsō* (往相), which means 'ascending phase.' In other words, one rises above one's individual consciousness and merges into oneness with the divine.

20. The term used in Japanese is *gensō* (還相), which means 'descending phase.' In other words, one's awakened self returns to the material plane to work for the awakening of others.

21..The Iroha Song and the Song of Bamboo are traditional Japanese songs that are considered to have spiritual significance.

22. The Shirahato Society was the women's group within Seicho-No-Ie.

23. *Namu-Amidabutsu* (南無阿弥陀仏) is a recitation introduced by the Buddhist priest Hōnen, founder of the *Jōdoshū* (浄土宗—Pure Land sect). The same recitation is used in the *Jōdoshinshū* (浄土真宗—New Pure Land sect), founded by the priest Shinran.

24. The *Kannon* (観音) Goddess is the Buddhist goddess of mercy, also known by the Sanskrit name *Avalokitesvara*. Refer to note 27.

25. A guardian divinity is a divine light, or angel, who is wholly dedicated to the guidance and protection of one human being. For details, refer to *God and Man* by Masahisa Goi (Byakko Press, 2005).

26. The *Nembutsu* (念仏) is the recitation of the phrase '*Namu-Amidabutsu*.' Refer to note 22.

27. *Kanzeon* (観世音) or *Kannon* (観音) is the Japanese name for the Bodhisattva of Compassion. The name may be translated as 'one who hears the cries of the world.' Refer to note 23.

28. The 'phenomenal self' refers not to the essential, divine self, but to the self as expressed through surface events and conditions (phenomena).

29. In Sanskrit, *bodhisattva* literally means 'being bent on enlightenment.' In Buddhist thought, it refers to one who is working not only for one's own enlightenment, but for the awakening of all people.

30. At present, this would have the spending power of about US $100.

31. The term used in the original is 'Sakyamuni.'

32. This likely refers to the phrase as it appears in the Lord's Prayer, although it is not certain.

33. The Ryūgū Palace (竜宮城—literally 'Dragon King's Court') appears in Japanese traditional literature. It is said to be located at the bottom of the sea near the Ryukyu Islands of Okinawa.

34. In Buddhist tradition, the *Nyoi-hōju* (如意宝珠) is a precious, sacred sphere that symbolizes the power of the divine world to purify illness and bring many kinds of blessings to the people of this world.

35. *Sakaki* (榊—Cleyera japonica) is an evergreen tree of the tea family that is often found in Japanese traditional stories, literature, and sacred rituals.

36. 'Subconscious embodiments' refers to ethereal, or astral, embodiments.

37. For a detailed explanation of 'the divine light of our original being,' called *Chokurei* (直霊), refer to *God and Man* by Masahisa Goi.

38. The phrase used in the original is: 'the realm transcending the three worlds (the world of greedy desires, the world of material substances, and the world of thoughts).' According to the teachings of Buddhism, human beings experience many births and rebirths within the confines of this realm of the three worlds, until they awaken to their divinity.

39. 'Returning from divine oneness' is the same as the 'descending phase' (*gensō*) described in note 19.

40. Shōnkaku was a private commercial property located in Ichikawa, Chiba Prefecture, and it became the Shinden (新田) Dōjō. A *dōjō* (道場) is a hall used for meditation,

martial arts, or other forms of training. The first character means 'path,' while the second character means 'place.' Thus, a *dōjō* is a place where one practices a particular path, or way, toward spiritual development.

41. In Japan, for most marriages there are two ceremonies: a legal one and a social one. The legal one is the official registration of the marriage, which the couple do at the city office. The social one is where the couple, accompanied by their go-betweens and close family members, announce their marriage to relatives, friends, and acquaintances. The social ceremony is usually preceded by a small religious ceremony, held on the same day.

42. *IN* (印) is a Japanese word similar in meaning to the Sanskrit word *mudra*. It consists of hand movements, peaceful breathing, and vocal sounds that attune us to the universal laws of harmony.

A Message to Our Readers

In 1955, the same year he wrote this book, Masahisa Goi initiated a worldwide movement of prayer for world peace, based on the peace prayer and message 'May Peace Prevail on Earth.'

Several organizations have formed themselves around Mr. Goi's vision for peace, including Byakko Shinko Kai, the World Peace Prayer Society, and the Goi Peace Foundation. Interested people may contact these organizations for further information. The addresses are shown below:

Byakko Shinko Kai

A worldwide grassroots peace initiative aimed at assisting all people in furthering their highest spiritual aspirations and goals.

812-1 Hitoana, Fujinomiya, Shizuoka 418-0102 Japan

Phone +81 (0)544 29 5100 Fax +81 (0)544 29 5111

E-mail: e-info@byakkopress.ne.jp

http://www.byakko.org

http://www.byakkopress.ne.jp

The World Peace Prayer Society

A Non-Governmental Organization (NGO) associated with the
Dept. of Public Information at the United Nations;
dedicated to spreading the non-sectarian message and prayer
'May Peace Prevail on Earth.'
26 Benton Road, Wassaic, NY 12592 USA
E-mail: info@worldpeace.org
http://www.worldpeace.org

The Goi Peace Foundation

Working to build a global peace network uniting our hearts and
our wisdom for world peace; established in Tokyo with the ap-
proval of the Japanese Ministry of Education.
Heiwa Daiichi Bldg. 1-4-5 Hirakawa-cho
Chiyoda-ku, Tokyo 102-0093 Japan
Phone +81 (0)3 3265 2071 Fax +81 (0)3 3239 0919
E-mail: info@goipeace.or.jp
http://www.goipeace.or.jp

May Peace Prevail on Earth

天と地をつなぐ者 (One Who Unites Heaven and Earth)

2005年 12月 1日　初版
2008年 5月 1日　二版

著者　　五井昌久
英訳者　小林絵理奈、ジュディス・ハント、スティーブンソン晶子、
　　　　高木俊介、立間紀子、田中園子、浜谷絹子、
　　　　フミ・ジョーンズ・スチュワート
監訳　　メアリ・マクエイド
発行者　平本雅登
発行所　白光真宏会出版本部 (白光出版)
　　　　〒418-0102静岡県富士宮市人穴812-1
　　　　(直販) 電話　0544 (29) 5109　FAX　0544 (29) 5122
　　　　(編集) 電話　0544 (29) 5106　FAX　0544 (29) 5116
　　　　ホームページ　http://www.byakkopress.ne.jp

東京出張所
〒101-0064東京都千代田区猿楽町2-1-16下平ビル401
　(営業) 電話　03 (5283) 5798　FAX　03 (5283) 5799

印刷所 Booksurge.com
ISBN 4-89214-166-6

Made in the USA
Monee, IL
17 December 2023

48930969R00118